Beat The **Bastard* Casinos

Pre-Setting Dice

***I Beat The Bastards,
So Can You ! ! !***

by Zeke Feinberg

All correspondence and inquiries should be directed to:

Reference Division
Hi-Lo-Yo Publishing Co.
P.O. Box 3066
Margate, N.J. 08402-3066

Library of Congress Cataloging in Publication Data Main entry under title: "BEAT THE *BASTARD CASINOS BY PRE-SETTING DICE"

Library of Congress Catalog Card Number: 92-072610
ISBN: 1-881174-05-0

Printed in the United States of America

TABLE OF CONTENTS

This book was
written in
SPITE OF MANY ! ! !

The Author

My family still does not approve of subject matter, and thinks I am too critical of casino personnel.

NOT A CONTROVERSIAL SUBJECT

Pre-Setting Dice is NOT a CONTROVERSIAL SUBJECT if you ask any of the KNOWNOTHINGISM EMPLOYEES OF CASINOS.

Every one of over many thousands of casino subjects stated emphatically that pre-setting dice when shooting has no effect on the outcome.

Not one Casino Employee agreed that pre-setting dice could result in profitable results.

Apologetic Corrections: Author interviewed a present Mirage (Las Vegas) CRAP DEALER who is firmly convinced he can control the outcome of a shooter's toss. If the shooter would toss the DICE as they were placed in front of the shooter, then the frequency of sevens or certain numbers could be altered. When exceptionally larger wagers were being pressed on a rare long hot streak, this particular dealer (stickperson extraordinaire) was brought in to increase the frequency of the killer seven. Conversely when a friendly crowd of decent tippers (tokes) for the dealers were overly generous, it was not unusual for this particular dealer to present the shooter with a pre-determined pre-set that would have a lesser frequency of sevens, therefore, more place bet and point numbers would be produced. The casinos never became burnt or were hurt since time and action consumed the major share of the available CRAP bankroll (over 34 %).

A former Atlantic City CRAP dealer, Bob Mera, became a successful entrepreneur specializing in gambling merchandise, gambling books and trinkets. His Gaming Emporium is located in Ocean One, Atlantic City. The inventory of gambling paraphernalia is extensive. So is his gambling knowledge. For more information about the Gaming Emporium call 800-345-3075.

Bob Mera exposed his primary function, when in the role of stickperson, during a recent interview.

Like the Mirage stickperson, the pit bosses used Bob Mera's "talents" to stop those rare hot streaks when unusually large sums were being placed in jeopardy's way. We discussed the expected results for certain pre-sets. By results it is meant the anticipated alteration in the frequency table. Yes, our retired stickperson was convincingly certain that under certain conditions the Arena of CRAP Action was under his control when in the role of stickperson.

My interest in pre-setting DICE was inspired by MANY shooters obtaining 7's and 11's on the come-out-rolls at a frequency dramatically higher than theoretically expected on a consistent basis.

This interest was further enhanced when a math professor at two New Jersey universities suggested that the frequency of sevens could be lessened if the DICE were thrown from a certain "position". This math professor should have further explored his suggestion, but it would have interfered with his addiction. Two math faculty positions (day & night) were necessary to monetarily feed his addiction to the game of CRAPS, especially since the Atlantic City casinos were within reasonable driving time.

This particular very knowledgeable math professor ranks as one of the Palladium of CRAP Action's WORST CRAP PLAYERS.

In fact, three other math professors with whom I became friendly never fully comprehended the sixth grade arithmetic of CRAPS. No wonder the U.S.A. ranked 5th in a world comparison of math knowledge for our university students.

Korea was number one, and we Americans were a dismal fifth. Allow a little digression time. The fault is not with our intelligence, but with the ability of our teachers. Good teachers deserve superior salaries, but most deserve subnormal salaries for their end results. My superior math knowledge is not because of my intelligence, but because of certain teachers and professors who taught and influenced with unusual talent.

Pardon me, but I had to get if off my chest. Onward !

Let me take you through the process that led to a "scientific" analysis of pre-setting DICE.

I picked up a pair of DICE and started to analyze one DIE (singular of DICE). In how many positions could this singular DIE be placed ?

This is a cube (six sides). Each side is numbered from one dot (1) to six dots (6). The opposite sides of any DIE always add up to seven (7).

Let's place one dot (1) as the uppermost flat surface. The bottom surface must be the complement (6 dots) to make a total of seven (7). Therefore the remaining four sides would comprise the other numbers or dots (2, 3, 4 and 5).

The four positions possible with one dot (1) on the top surface would be:

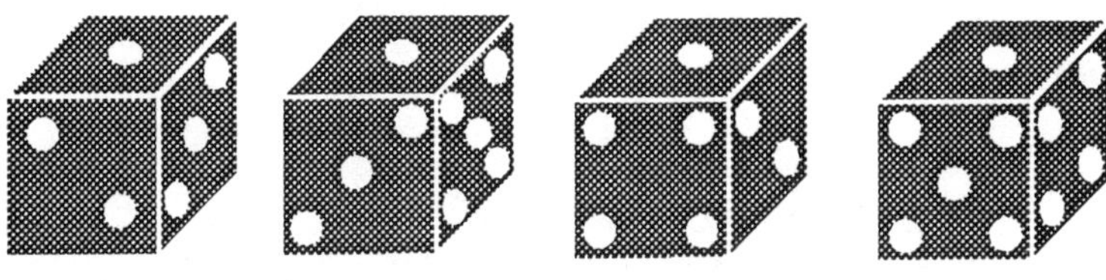

Once these DICE are positioned as shown, remember that dots on opposite sides add up to seven. Therefore, once a DIE is positioned with a particular number of dots on top surface and a specific number is on the vertical surface facing the shooter, then all six faces are fixed with a definite value.

Let's take a DIE with the one dot on the top surface and two dots on the front surface facing the shooter. Place an imaginary horizontal axle through the two opposite sides containing three dots (3) and four dots (4).

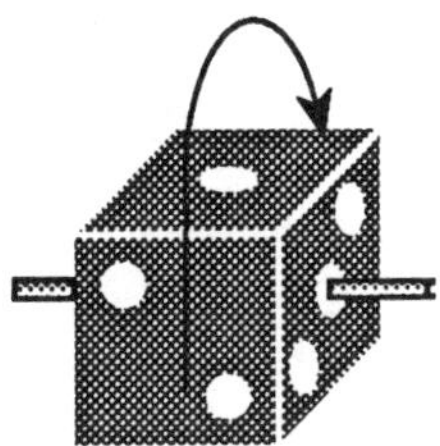

Let's rotate the DIE clockwise on this imaginary axle. What do we observe Only the one, two, six and five will appear. The three and four cannot appear.

If we were to add a second DIE (now a pair of DICE) to the axle, in the same exact position as the first, we learn something new.

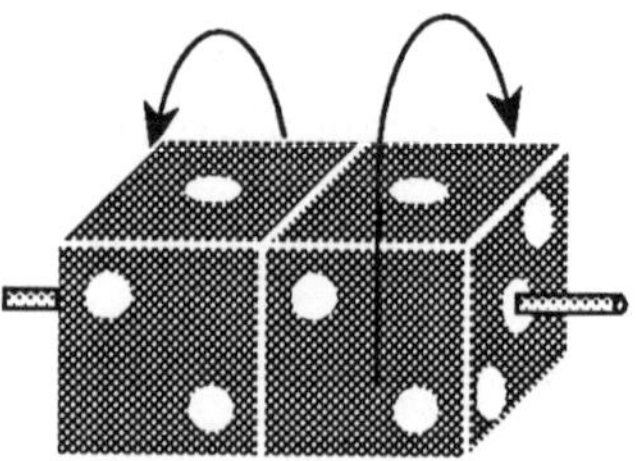

Lets rotate these two Die independently of each other. The only possible number combinations on top surface are:

1 - 1	2 - 1	6 - 1	5 - 1
1 - 2	2 - 2	6 - 2	5 - 2
1 - 6	2 - 6	6 - 6	5 - 6
1 - 5	2 - 5	6 - 5	5 - 5

Mathematically, the sixteen possible combinations are correct. For any given number of the 1st Die there would be 4 possibilities on the 2nd Die. Therefore, the 4 possible numbers on the 1st Die would each have 4 possible combinations. Multiplication is really only adding many times the number being multiplied.

Can we obtain further knowledge from these 16 combinations ?

ABSOLUTELY ! ! !

Let's add up the various totals from the 16 possibilities.

1 + 1 = 2	2 + 1 = 3	6 + 1 = 7	5 + 1 = 6
1 + 2 = 3	2 + 2 = 4	6 + 2 = 8	5 + 2 = 7
1 + 6 = 7	2 + 6 = 8	6 + 6 = 12	5 + 6 = 11
1 + 5 = 6	2 + 5 = 7	6 + 5 = 11	5 + 5 = 10

Let's now notice how many times the total number can repeat itself within the 16 possibilities.

Frequency for DICE Totals

DICE Total		Frequency
2	-	1
3	-	2
4	-	1
5	-	0
6	-	2
7	-	4
8	-	2
9	-	0
10	-	1
11	-	2
12	-	1
		16 Possible DICE Totals

Please note there are theoretically no 5's or 9's, but four 7's.

It is obvious that when the top surface has one dot, that the vertical surface CANNOT BE one dot or six dots. All opposite sides of DICE must add up to seven (7). Therefore for a given top surface value (1, 2, 3, 4, 5 or 6) there will be only four vertical possibilities. The number value of the top surface cannot be repeated on the vertical surface.

Lets rotate the dice about on an imaginary vertical axis. You will notice...

if the **Top Surface** is:	1	1	1	1
then the **Front Surface** is:	2	3	5	4
Top Surface:	2	2	2	2
Front Surface:	1	4	6	3
Top Surface:	3	3	3	3
Front Surface:	1	2	6	5
Top Surface:	4	4	4	4
Front Surface:	1	5	6	2
Top Surface:	5	5	5	5
Front Surface:	1	3	6	4
Top surface:	6	6	6	6
Front Surface:	2	4	5	3

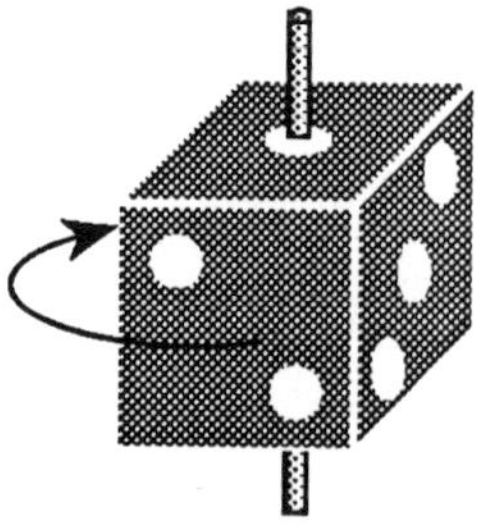

There are twenty-four possible pre-set combinations. Remember that the opposite sides must always total seven (7).

EXAMPLE:

Top Surface	1	1	1	1
Front Surface	2	3	4	5
Bottom Surface	6	6	6	6
Back Surface	5	4	3	2

Top Surface plus Bottom Surface = 7
Front Surface plus Back Surface = 7

24 POSSIBLE DICE SETTINGS

The twenty-four possible pre-sets have a very unusual make-up. Actually these twenty-four pre-set possible combinations are repeats of only ***three basic combinations*** (A, B, & C).

A = 1 - 2 - 6 - 5
B = 1 - 3 - 6 - 4
C = 2 - 3 - 5 - 4

As you can see on page 12, there are eight possible dice settings for each of these ***three basic combinations.***

How can we take advantage of this knowledge ?

Okay, so we know that there are twenty-four (24) possible combination pre-sets, and these are really variations of the ***three basic combinations.***

Ask yourself "How can I use this information to make profits and win at the CRAP table using dice that are erratic and crazy ?"

The answer will follow.

Now we are on the right track. Track number one (won) heading straight for the casino's cashiers cage.

The fuel we need for our train in order to continue to the cashier's cage is MORE KNOWLEDGE.

But remember: **when profits abound we must AVOID GREED, and be SELF-DISCIPLINED ! ! !**

BE PATIENT. Before heading for your favorite Arena of CRAP Action, additional knowledge is needed to combat the casino's win percentages that lead to a predatory money devouring conclusion.

Let's structure the twenty-four possible pre-sets showing the four surfaces except the two end surfaces:

	A	B	B	A	Combination
Top Surface:	1	1	1	1	
*Front Surface:	2	3	4	5	
Bottom Surface:	6	6	6	6	
Back Surface:	5	4	3	2	

	A	C	C	A	Combination
Top Surface:	2	2	2	2	
Front Surface:	1	3	4	6	
Bottom Surface:	5	5	5	5	
Back Surface:	6	4	3	1	

	B	C	C	B	Combination
Top Surface:	3	3	3	3	
Front Surface:	1	2	5	6	
Bottom Surface:	4	4	4	4	
Back Surface:	6	5	2	1	

	B	C	C	B	Combination
Top Surface:	4	4	4	4	
Front Surface:	1	2	5	6	
Bottom Surface:	3	3	3	3	
Back Surface:	6	5	2	1	

	A	C	C	A	Combination
Top Surface:	5	5	5	5	
Front Surface:	1	3	4	6	
Bottom Surface:	2	2	2	2	
Back Surface:	6	4	3	1	

	A	B	B	A	Combination
Top Surface:	6	6	6	6	
Front Surface:	2	3	4	5	
Bottom Surface:	1	1	1	1	
Back Surface:	5	4	3	2	

* For simplicity numbers are in value order, NOT rotation sequence. It is easier to comprehend.

Putting Knowledge To Use

We know the twenty-four (24) different positions that any two DICE can be positioned is really a derivative of **three basic combinations** that can be assembled in exactly six arrangements.

SIX POSSIBLE ARRANGEMENTS:

1st Die - 2nd Die

A - A
B - B
C - C
A - B
A - C
B - C

How does each of the six possible arrangements differ or vary from each other ? We are still analyzing everything; analytically and scientifically under IDEAL CONDITIONS. We are not in actual practice, yet, but will place each of these six combinations on an axle for theoretical answers.

Again let's repeat the three basic combinations

BASIC COMBINATIONS for each DIE:

Combination A = numbers (1 - 2 - 6 - 5)
Combination B = numbers (1 - 3 - 6 - 4)
Combination C = numbers (2 - 3 - 5 - 4)

Lets proceed and learn how various arrangements affect the frequency of Dice totals when tossed.

Appearance Frequency Of Dice Totals With Different Arrangement Combinations

To analyze what DICE TOTALS can be obtained, and how often the same total will appear, let's place these arrangements on the axle and rotate the Dice so different numbers appear on top. There are 16 possible combinations that equal the Dice totals.

(To obtain the Dice Totals rotate the Dice independently of each other. The result will be a new number on the top surface.)

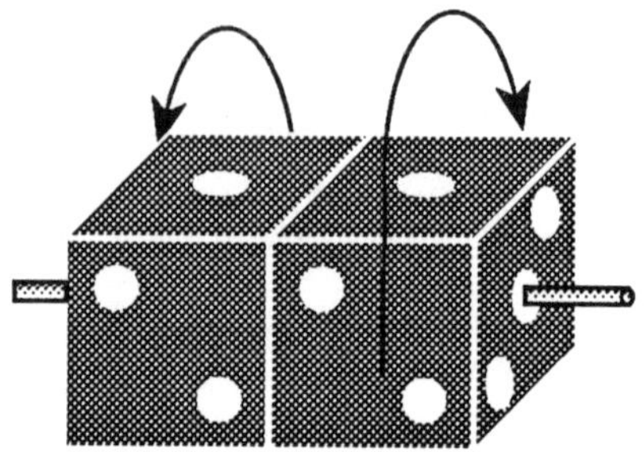

A - A Arrangement

1st Die (A)	2nd Die (A)	Dice Total	*Appearance Frequency
1	1	2	1
2	2	3	2
6	6	4	1
5	5	5	0
		6	2
		7	4
		8	2
		9	0
		10	1
		11	2
		12	1
			16

Note: No theoretical 5's or 9's. Four possible 7's. Super pre-set for horns, whirls and 7's. Right and Wrong bettor would naturally use the abundance of 7's differently. Very bad for Place bet numbers. Excellent for hardway numbers.

Zeke's favorite: For come out rolls only. Super for Wrong bettor after point is established, so *beware of shooter's pre-set.*

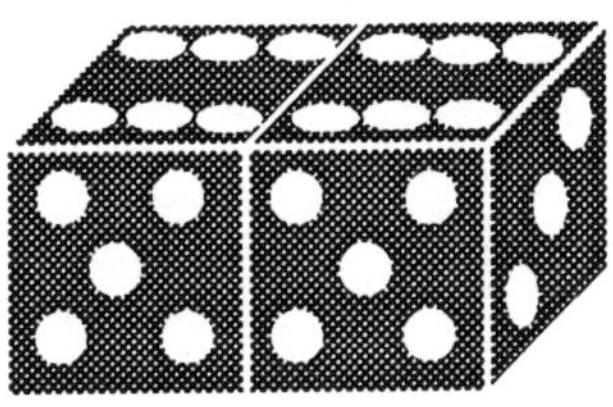

* Appearance Frequency is the number of times a particular Dice total will appear by rotating the dice independently of each other. Example: Using the A-A combination, the 8 can appear only twice (a 6 & 2 and a 2 & 6).

B - B Arrangement

1st Die (B)	2nd Die (B)	Dice Totals	Appearance Frequency
1	1	2	1
3	3	3	0
6	6	4	2
4	4	5	2
		6	1
		7	4
		8	1
		9	2
		10	2
		11	0
		12	1
			16

Note: No treys (ace-duce 1-2) or yo's (eleven). Four possible 7's. Ten out of sixteen place bet numbers. Better for outside numbers (4, 5, 9, 10) than the 6 and 8. Less opportunity for craps on come out roll (2 out of 16 possibilities). Very bad for hardways.

Zeke's favorite: ***None***

C - C Arrangement

1st Die (C)	2nd Die (C)	Dice Totals	Appearance Frequency
2	2	2	0
3	3	3	0
5	5	4	1
4	4	5	2
		6	3
		7	4
		8	3
		9	2
		10	1
		11	0
		12	0
			16

Note: No Crap numbers, No yo's (elevens). Possibility of four 7's. Super for hardways. Great if you desire less Crap numbers. Excellent for Place bets, but the 7's can kill you. Twelve Place bet numbers and also four 7's. Better 6 and 8 opportunities.

Zekes Favorite: A long tine favorite that's sometime confusing. Good for come out rolls with the hardways in action (working). Naturally you should place an equivalent hardways wager on the 7. I have experienced many unusually long series of Pass line wins. At other times the 7 is the prevalent killer. I suggest experimenting, but tread lightly.

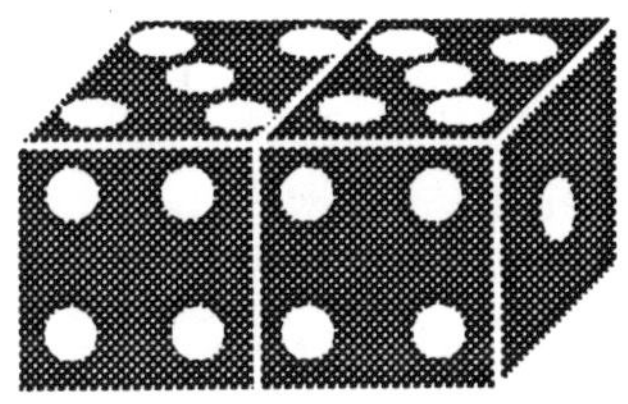

A - B Arrangement

1st Die (A)	2nd Die (B)	Dice Total	Appearance Frequency
1	1	2	1
2	3	3	1
6	6	4	1
5	4	5	2
		6	2
		7	2
		8	2
		9	2
		10	1
		11	1
		12	1
			16

Note: Fair for horns and whirls. Only two possible 7's. Ten theoretical place bet numbers out of theoretical sixteen. Super for inside numbers (5, 6, 8, 9). Horrible for hardways. Good for whirls and horns.

Zeke's Favorite: (rare)

A -C Arrangement

1st Die (A)	2nd Die (C)	Dice Totals	Appearance Frequency
1	2	2	0
2	3	3	1
6	5	4	2
5	4	5	2
		6	2
		7	2
		8	2
		9	2
		10	2
		11	1
		12	0
			16

Note: No hi-lo's (12, 2). Only two possible 7's. Excellent for place bets - Twelve out of sixteen theoretical possibilities. Hardways 4's and 10's.

Zeke's favorite:

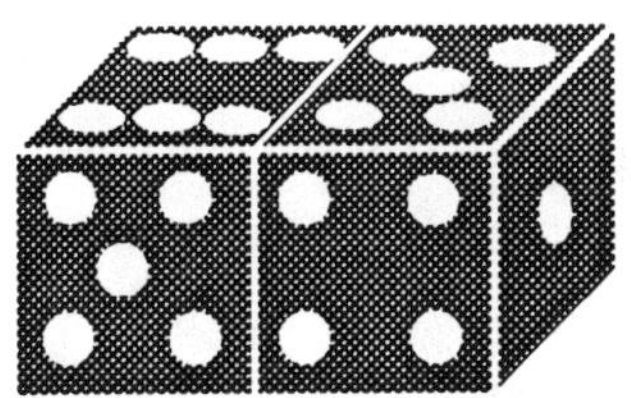

B -C Arrangement

1st Die (B)	2nd Die (C)	Dice Total	Appearance Frequency
1	2	2	0
3	3	3	1
6	5	4	1
4	4	5	2
		6	3
		7	2
		8	3
		9	2
		10	1
		11	1
		12	0
			16

Note: No hi-lo's (12, 2). Only two possible 7's. Twelve place numbers, six being the 6 and 8. Super for inside numbers (5, 6, 8, 9).

Zeke's favorites:

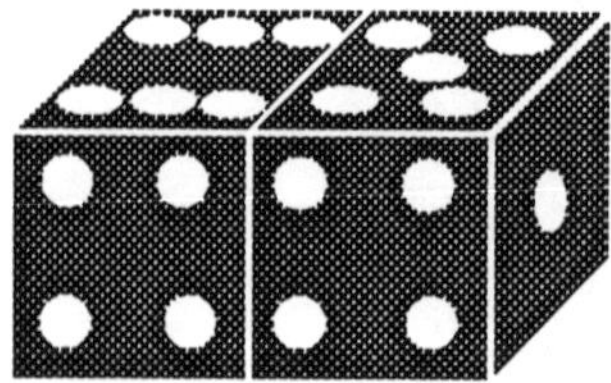

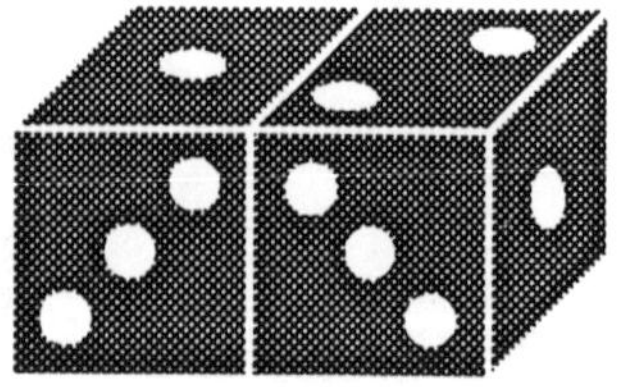

Now that we have obtained the hypothetical combinations, let's condense the results of all six arrangements. Don't forget these values were obtained from a fixed axle condition that *did not* allow the two end DICE numbers to be involved in the results. The information regarding the frequency of possible numbers will be very useful in the profitable future.

FREQUENCY OF NUMBERS USING VARIOUS BASIC PRE-SET COMBINATIONS

Number	*A - A*	*B - B*	*C - C*	*A - B*	*A - C*	*B - C*
2	1	1	0	1	0	0
3	2	0	0	1	1	1
4	1	2	1	1	2	1
5	0	2	2	2	2	2
6	2	1	3	2	2	3
7	4	4	4	2	2	2
8	2	1	3	2	2	3
9	0	2	2	2	2	2
10	1	2	1	1	2	1
11	2	0	0	1	1	1
12	1	1	0	1	0	0
	16	16	16	16	16	16

We have found a logical scientific basis that each pre-set has definitive theoretical values. We now must proceed in two different directions — fortunately not at the same time.

First we must determine how to take advantage of the different characteristics obtained when intermingling the Basic Combinations.

Finally, the ultimate test would be to put into profitable practice our theoretical knowledge. It is not as difficult as one may think.

Before going into specific details let's discuss the variety of conditions that can be explored when two different or same Basic Combinations are used:

- (a) *More Sevens*
- (c) *More Horn or Whirl Numbers*
- (d) *More Inside Numbers*
- (e) *More 6's and 8's*
- (f) *More Hardway Numbers*
- (g) *Even Distribution for the Six Place Bet Numbers*
- (h) *etc . . .*

Before we proceed, beware of other people's pre-sets. Some shooters unknowingly have pre-sets that are more prone to generate more sevens. An intelligent high roller wrong bettor can have a confederate co-player attempt to create a 7 once the point number is established.

Most shooters do not change the setting of the DICE as they are offered by the stickperson. This can have tendencies to assist winning your wagers or jeopardizing them. We will expand on this subject later.

ZEKE'S FAVORITE PRE-SETS

COME-OUT-ROLL PRE-SETS

*This is the **A - A** Combination*

Sevens: 4 out of 16 possibilities
Whirls: 10 out of 16 possibilities
Horns: 6 out of 16 possibilililties
Hardways: 2 (4 and 10)

ONCE A POINT NUMBER IS ESTABLISHED

More Inside Numbers (5, 6, 8, 9)

*This is the **B - C** Combination*

Sevens: 2 out of 16 possibilities
Inside Numbers: (5, 6, 8, 9) 10 out of 16 possibilities
Six and Eight: (6, 8) 6 out of 16 possibilities

Only one CRAP number (3)

ONCE POINT NUMBER IS ESTABLISHED

FOR ALL SIX PLACE BETS

*This is the **A - C** Combination*

Sevens: 2 out of 16 possibilities
Inside Numbers: 8 out of 16 possibilities
Six Place Bet Numbers: 12 out of 16 possibilities
Hardways: 2 (4 and 10)

HARDWAY NUMBERS

*This is the **C - C** Combination*

Sevens:	4 out of 16 possibilities
Inside Numbers:	(5, 6, 8, 9) 10 out of 16 possibilities
Six Place Bets:	12 out of 16 possibilities
Hardways:	4 out of 16 possibilities

Crap Numbers: 0 — **Yes, Zero**

Excellent for working on come out roll, in spite of four 7's. When shooting on come out roll make certain that pass line wager offsets hardway wagers, or have a chip wager on the "any seven" equivalent to the chip wager on one of the hardway numbers.

Treacherous pre-set once point number is established.

CAUTION

Pre-Sets tend to change the frequency of certain numbers. This does not mean that certain specific numbers may appear more than theoretically expected or less than theoretically expected. Sometimes everything goes awry. Other times this altering of the frequency is unbelievably on target.

I have emphatically stated that over a fairly long period of time, these alterations of the 36 Probability Table will work to the shooters profitable advantage.

ANY PARTICULAR BASIC PRE-SET

Let's take any one Basic Pre-Set as an example. It can be any of the three basic pre-sets. Look at the "B" combination (1, 3, 6, 4) for one die. In theory, this combination (1, 3, 6, 4) will rotate about the imaginary axis between the two vertical faces of 2 and 5.

This statement is most important. Any set-up of these four numbers can be used as long as the two numbers for the top vertical surface and front surface are adjoining numbers.

The adjoining numbers are:

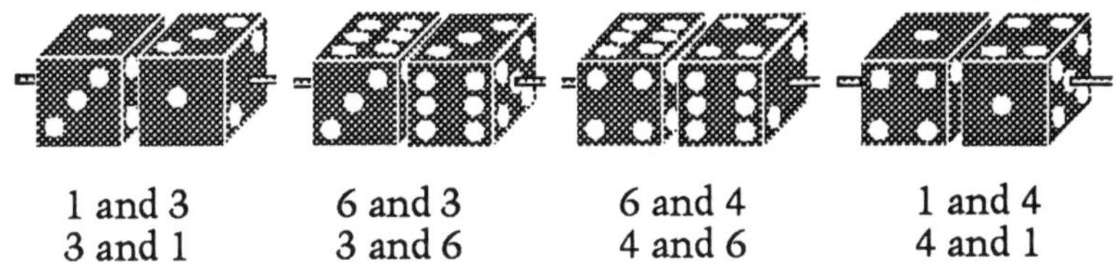

1 and 3	6 and 3	6 and 4	1 and 4
3 and 1	3 and 6	4 and 6	4 and 1

A total of eight different set-ups

Therefore this "B" die can be pre-set in any of the eight above set-ups. Assembling two DICE in preparation for a pre-set has many possibilities. Each DIE has eight possible settings. Therefore there are 64 possible pre-sets available. Time is limited (at the CRAP table) and can be very expensive, even if only wagering on the pass line (or don't pass line).

I suggest experimenting with only a few until the results make you feel comfortable or use Zeke's Best Pre-Sets, until you find some that work better for you. I am fairly certain that any one of the many basic combinations will do the job for which it is intended.

This author has not exposed many dollars to come up with Zeke's best pre-sets. Neither should you. I found my preferred pre-sets fairly quickly, and so should you.

More importantly shoot on a not-so-crowded CRAP table. With crowded CRAP tables, the desired same position is not always available. It seems not to matter when the pre-sets are on target. Any position is profitable. When the seven erupts unexpectedly once the point number is established it could occur from any position on the table.

I have had best results when my motion of tossing is smooth and fairly constant at any position of the small table. Never force a throw. Don't be concerned with the DICE bouncing off the padded front wall. Don't throw too hard, but toss firmly and let the pre-sets develop. True that sometimes bad things develop. Again sometimes you can't produce a mistake (7) no matter how you toss the DICE, but overall you will be a winner.

Try it...

You will like it ! ! !

You will earn money going for one or two place bet wins. Using intelligent pre-sets with a good tossing format should give you unusual profitable results.

Be patient ! ! !

Be self disciplined ! ! !

Don't be greedy ! ! !

As an experienced pre-set shooter, instead of your pass line wager losing 59.39 % of the time (after the point number is established) you will be **winning** the point number wager MORE than 50 % of the time. This is a by-product of more numbers being generated due to your selected pre-set. Transforming the point number into more than a 50 % winner compared to the theoretical 59.39 % loser is a dramatic increase in profitability.

For super best results combine pre-set knowledge along with the knowledge learned from either of my other books:

"Earn $12 to $24 Each Hour Playing Casino Craps"

"Casino Craps is a $$ Devouring Casino Game"

STICKPERSON: FRIEND OR FOE ?

WITH VERY, VERY, VERY RARE EXCEPTION, MOST STICKPERSONS DO NOT BELIEVE THAT ANY PRE-SET OF THE DICE ALTERS THE OUTCOME OF THE SHOOTER'S TOSS.

Author's Statement: Twenty minutes of each hour of every working day, every Crap Dealer in the Arena of CRAP Action takes on the role of Stickperson, for the sole purpose of passing time.

This is not to slight their work habits. It is my opinion that ninety-five plus percent (95 %) of these stickpersons are adept and very efficient in their duties.

Less than five (5 %) percent are so-so and are derelict in the performance of their duties as they go through the machinations of stickperson's duties.

You would think that at least some of these dealers, when in the role of stickperson, would experiment intellectually to make the role of stickperson more interesting. Try presenting various pre-sets and observe what occurs. Stickpeople consider their well paid (thanks to tokes) work as most boring.

Most CRAP Shooters do NOT PRE-SET the DICE prior to shooting. Those that do pre-set the DICE do so WITHOUT ANY KNOWLEDGE, only a hope and a prayer.

Most stickpersons, when they place the DICE in front of the shooter, for a come-out-roll will have on the top two flat surfaces — a total of 7 or 11, never a 2, 3 or 12.

Once the point number is established the stickperson will generally place in front of the shooter a total equal to the point number, or the total on the opposite sides of the DICE. If the point number is 4 the shooter may be presented with the 4 or 10 on the top surfaces. For the 6 point it could be either the 6 or 8 on the top surfaces; the point number 5 would have the shooter with the totals 5 or 9 on the top surfaces, etc.

This author has NEVER WITNESSED a stickperson presenting the shooter with BOTH the top surfaces AND two vertical surfaces in a pre-determined pre-set condition.

Stickpersons generally will never offer the DICE with a 7 or Crap total on the top flat surfaces, once the point number is established.

Some more knowledgeable players have instructed the stickperson, "never give me the DICE with double numbers showing". Statements like this prove that some players have experienced desired and undesired results from certain "top-totals" on DICE. Yes, pre-sets have been around before this author was born.

An interesting analysis is shown on the following tabulation chart that indicated how 1738 CRAP players handled their shooting or non-shooting responsibilities:

RESULTS OF SHOOTER'S METHODS OF TOSSING DICE

Analysis was taken during 22 days that spanned more than 7 weeks.

Casino	*Observed Tables*	*Observed Players*
Bally Grand	26	211
Bally Park Place	14	124
Caesars	37	364
Claridge	16	129
Sands	28	198
Showboat	18	147
Trump's Plaza	16	163
Trump's Taj Mahal	39	402
	194	1738

Total Players	1738	
Passed DICE (non-shooters)	- 241	(unusually high, but accurate)
Shooters	1497	

Note: 172 of 241 non-shooters were "wrong players" wagering from "don't" side. Included in 1497 shooters were 33 "wrong players" and 23 of these tossed from the pass line, leaving 10 shooters from the don't side.

Tossed DICE as presented by stickperson:

Without "shaking" DICE	1167
"Shaking" DICE	184
* Pre-set and Tossed DICE	97
* Pre-set then shook DICE before tossing	49
Shooters	1497

* 146 (97 + 49) Players who pre-set were very inconsistent. Pre-Sets on come-out-rolls had top surfaces of 7, 11 and 12 primarily, with double numbers the next choice.

It appeared that only the pre-sets on come-out-rolls were deliberate. After point numbers were established most pre-setters did not use same top surface totals for every toss. It was too difficult to determine vertical faces but it appeared that pre-setters were only concerned with top flat surfaces. Perhaps 10 % of pre-setters were concerned with also pre-setting vertical faces, but this was too difficult to ascertain.

TOSSING THE DICE

In order to take advantage of the knowledge that certain basic combinations will enhance particular profitable phases in our Arena of CRAP Action, the shooter must toss the DICE in a manner to assist in a slight alteration of the frequency table.

All that is necessary to have the casino's win percentages go from a profitable plus to a negative casino's win percentage is a slight deviation from the frequency table. Repeat! Only a very slight deviation is necessary to cause you, the CRAP Player, to obtain a positive player's win percentage. Let's go through an example.

Assume that you are in the role of being the shooter. The dollar values used in this example will be the minimum allowed, but any multiple of these dollar values would result in higher dollar profits.

During a previous chapter we explained which pre-setting of the DICE is best for certain wagers.

Okay, let's proceed.

As a shooter, on the come-out-role, you place a $5 red chip on the pass line. "Five dollars for a whirl!"
Whirl wager is explained on page 35. A whirl wager is a one-time wager only valid for the very next toss of the DICE. It is known in the Arena of CRAP Action as a proposition bet. Normally all proposition wagers will eventually flush the player into the financial sewer.

BUT NOT FOR THE PRE-SETTER ! ! !

Procedure for Tossing Dice

Don't be afraid to toss DICE firmly (but not hard) against the opposite furthest wall from where you are standing. Hitting the wall with both DICE is a must in all casinos, and believe it or not, this does not work against the shooter.

First pre-set the DICE to the setting desired. Make certain that both DICE are firmly against each other.

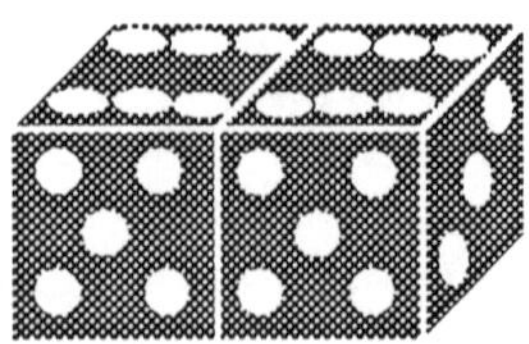

Pick up the DICE with two or three fingers on the back surfaces (in this case the 2 and 2) and the thumb on the front surfaces (in this case the 5 and 5). Remember the front surface faces shooter.

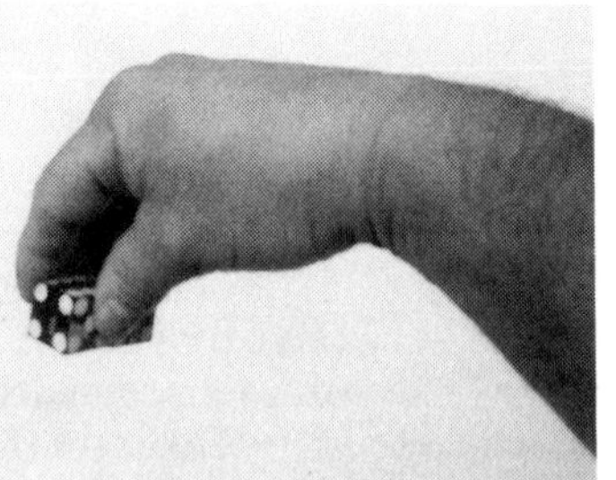

Note the downward bent wrist

Toss the DICE in an arc (3' to 4' high) against the padded wall with an outward flick of the wrist. This will cause the DICE to rotate in the air in a **Counter - Clockwise** rotation.

Fear not. We are not going to control the DICE but our effortless motion is all that is needed to ***alter the Frequency of the Dice Totals.***

The chaotic bouncing of the DICE will actually assist the shooter in the ***altering the DICE totals frequency.***

From Chaos Order Will Develop ! ! !

Avoid the corners of the wall. Try to toss the Dice between the players chips, so when they bounce off the wall, the chances of hitting obstacles are minimized. DICE bouncing off chips should be avoided.

Repeat: Never Toss Into The Far Corners

Just a light, but firm, flick of the wrist is all that's needed to send the DICE rotating in a ***Counter - Clockwise*** rotation.

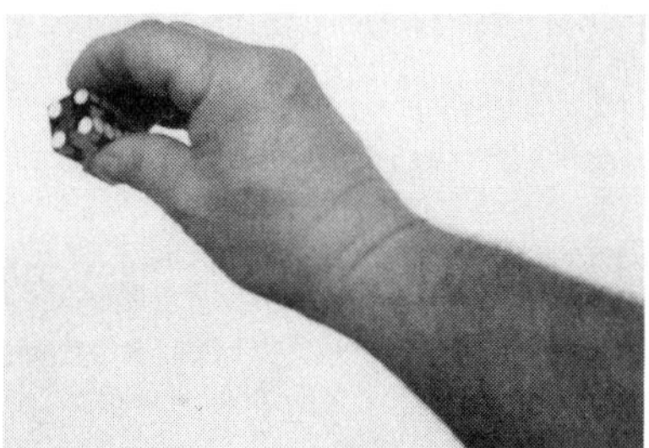

Note the upward bent wrist

Again -- fear not because with all the chaotic bouncing the procedure of pre-setting the Dice and properly tossing of the DICE will lead your wagers out of *temptation's way* more often than not.

Our minimum goal is four wins for every singular loss when place betting the four inside numbers (5, 6, 8, 9).

Chaotic bouncing will lead the shooter through an orderly process that results in Profits.

Important note: If as a shooter (on the small table, naturally) you are positioned immediately next to the stick person or in the position second to the stickperson, the tossing arc should be lower (2' to 3').

Zeke's comment: Believe me you can be successful more often than not. Our goal is profits with a pleasant smile, in a most exciting and exhilarating atmosphere.

VIGILANCE IN CRAPS

(1) **Beware** of any shooter, once the point number is established, who tosses either on purpose or unintentionally a pre-set with DICE values of sevens or CRAPS. This author's pre-set of acey-deuce (1-2) is an exception because of vertical pre-set, otherwise beware of any acey-deuce pre-set.

(2) Watch out for the shooter who merely picks up the DICE in the same format as presented by the stickperson. If this is the case then be on the alert for the habits of the stickperson in offering DICE to the shooter.

(3) The above cautions are sufficient in themselves to make decisions whether to allow place bets to be *"working"* or *"off"*, BUT two other tools will assist you in earning profits:

(a) *Charting (Super-charting and Mega- charting)

(b) Intuition

(4) Pre-Sets are more valid on small CRAP Tables and less effective on larger tables.

REWARD :

If you never toss the DICE but used your pre-set knowledge when others shoot then you are headed for that unusual post in the Arena of CRAP Action, ***that of a winner.***

* ***Charting is fully explained in this book***

WHIRL WAGERS

Whirls are wagered in increments of $5 (red chip). A basic $5 whirl means that $1 (white chip) is wagered on each of the following one-shot wagers:

Any Seven (7)	Natural	Pays 4 to 1
* Twelve (12)	Box Cars	Pays 30 to 1
* Aces (2)	Snake-Eyes	Pays 30 to 1
* Three (3)	Acey-Deuce	Pays 15 to 1
* Eleven (11)	Yo	Pays 15 to 1

* Atlantic City pay-off odds. Nevada and other states pay less.

Theoretical casino's win percentage for any whirl wager:

Ways to make a whirl out of the 36 Probability Table:

Number	Ways to Make
7	6
12	1
2	1
3	2
11	2

Ways to make	12
* Ways to lose	24
Total	36 Events

* Since the whirl is a one toss wager (one time only) then the other 24 possible numbers cause a loss.

Whirl Investment = 36 Tosses x $ 5 =		$ 180

* Return = Ways to make times payoff

Seven (7)	6 ways ($ 4 + $1) =	$ 30
Twelve (12)	1 way ($30 + $1) =	$ 31
Aces (2)	1 way ($30 + $1) =	$ 31
Three (3)	2 ways ($15 + $1) =	$ 32
Eleven (11)	2 ways ($16 + $1) =	$ 32

Return for Whirl =	$156	$156
Casino's Dollar Win		$ 24
Casino's Win Percentage		13.33 %

* Includes the win in dollars plus the return of the original wager. In other words the return for a 4 to 1 wager is 5.

To create a profit for the whirl bet the shooter must find a method to increase the dollar return by more than the normal loss of $24. Obviously the pre-setter must cause a greater return by creating more than theoretically expected whirl numbers.

After reviewing my personal chart records for one of my come-out-roll pre-sets my average whirl numbers generated per 36 come-out rolls are:

Number	Theoretical Frequency	Zeke's Frequency
7	6	9.0
12	1	1.6
2	1	1.2
3	2	2.3
11	2	2.1

Zeke's Investment:	36 x $ 5	=	$ 180.00

Zeke's Return:

Seven (7)	9 ways	($ 44 + $ 1)	=	45.00
Twelve (12)	1.6 ways	($ 30 + $ 1)	=	49.60
Aces (2)	1.2 ways	($ 30 + $ 1)	=	37.20
Three (3)	2.3 ways	($ 15 + $ 1)	=	36.90
Eleven (11)	2.1 ways	($ 15 + $ 1)	=	33.60
	Zeke's Return for Whirl			$ 202.20

Zeke's Dollar Win	$ 22.80
Zeke's Win Percentage	12.67 %

Actually over many periods this particular pre-set (6 over 5 and 6 over 5) has generated more than 3 twelves and 9 sevens per 36 tosses. The six would be the top flat surface and the five is the number of dots on the front surface facing you, the tosser.

Some people parley their horn or whirl wagers. I do not parley these wagers and recommend that you do not parley them. I generally will increase my wagers by at least the value of the original whirl wager. but not when the stickman's call is 7.

This illustration was not presented for profit seekers. I do so for diversion and fun time plus allowing the dealers to partake by making dealer wagers very often. One of my favorite dealer toke wagers is "one dollar for the dealers on the horn". This wager is only permissible for the dealers. The pay-offs to the dealers are either $4 and down or $8 and down. This author always renews the dealer's horn wager after a win.

This is really an exercise for my ego — having the ability to alter the frequency table to favor my wagers.

You can add profits on the come out roll by placing a $1 unit for any CRAPS for every $5 on the pass line, when using the 6 over 5 and 6 over 5 pre-set.

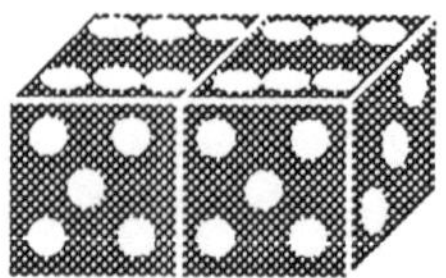

Before it is shown how to generate LESS sevens and more place bet (or point) numbers, let's review one of my favorite profitable pre-set endeavors — the HARDWAYS.

Fortunately for me and unfortunately for the casinos there are basically three different pre-sets that assisted me in winning el dinero from the casinos. All three pre-sets for the hardways will be revealed in this book.

There are four hardway numbers theoretically per 36 Frequency Table. What does it take for the shooter to create profits instead of losing money playing the hardways ? Allow this author to short-cut the answer. All of the 6th grade arithmetic is in the "Hardway" chapter of another book*.

Using Atlantic City's hardway pay-offs, or the lower Las Vegas pay-offs, if only one more hardway per 36 Probability Table (five instead of theoretical four) is generated, then profits are assured. From empirical action five to six hardways per 36 tosses is not unusual, with Pre-sets.

Again I consider profits on the hardways as fun time.

Beating the smarty casinos is easier and more profitable by obtaining more place bet numbers when shooting. This will be the thrust for profit making. Yes, more place bet numbers.

This author is convinced that profits are earned by playing the place bet numbers intelligently. Pre-Setting the DICE for more place bet numbers is adding insurance for our profit-making. You the player should be patient, self disciplined and not greedy, even with cooperating pre-sets.

* "Hardways, Horns, Craps and Hi-Lo-Yo."

16 VERSUS 36

The six pre-set combinations only depict total possible DICE totals of 16 instead of 36. This occurs because the two vertical end faces of each DIE are fixed because of the axle being placed between these ends.

In practice (for real money) the DICE are not restrained and 36 DICE totals are possible. The question in our minds would be: "Is there a relationship between the two situations, one where only 16 DICE totals are possible and the 36 possible DICE totals in live action ?"

This author believes there is a "relationship". Talk is cheap. The proof of the pudding is profits.

If the back padded wall of our sacred CRAP Table was flat, there would be no question that a desired DICE total would alter tremendously in favor of the shooter's pre-set characteristic.

BUT the furthest table wall is NOT flat. Instead it has a specially designed pattern to thwart any "controlled" DICE action. The DICE will bounce everywhere with no sense of direction.

Back to the pudding test — profits. Even before I became interested in studying the game of CRAPS, I played CRAPS for very small sums primarily for entertainment.

It was obvious to me that sometimes, certain shooters, had the knack of producing more 7's and 11's on the come-out-roll than the frequency table suggested.

Having two manufacturing facilities in the Los angeles environment and one in Kingman, Arizona, stopping in Las Vegas when traveling to and from Philadelphia International Airport was very convenient. Since 1953 over 400 such "drop-ins" occurred. I spent alot of time in the casino, either playing low level games (sometimes 25 cent minimum) or watching real action. Even then I noticed that 95 % of those in the Palatial Arena of High Rollers played the same stupid way. Even then I thought that these losers were poor students of the game.

During the past fifteen to eighteen years I would chart ONLY the flow of tossed numbers and the decisions. So I had sufficient retained paper work to review for certain conditions. Unfortunately in the earlier years of charting I did not make any notations regarding hardways or superstitious outcomes as the DICE went flying hither, thither and yon.

During travel time I would review these charts. And even then I pondered why periodically on the come-out rolls the frequency of the 7's and 11's appeared out of bounds on the very high side. Though I noticed this phenomenon periodically it was dismissed as one of those typical random flow of numbers. I later retrieved some very old records plus the latest charts and observed that the same shooters at the same table were having this unusual luck. It was easy, sometimes to review the charts and from the flow of decisions approximate whether or not the same shooters prevailed with lucky 7's and 11's. Honestly, the margin of error in distinguishing the same shooter is asinine. It could be 50 % or higher, but still worthwhile. Weird interpretation, but possible.

Since July 1990 I pondered the question , "Can the DICE be somewhat controlled ?"

My conclusion is that NO ONE can absolutely or partially control the outcome of the stickman's call. After considerable thought I believed that conditions could be altered.

I made a positive effort to go to a CRAP Table where I could shoot more frequently or be the only shooter (especially when new tables open up) or go from table to table after leaving one as the last shooter. This was very costly in order to experiment. I copied other shooter's pre-sets and mostly contrived my own. The only good thing financially was that in those days (1990 and 1991) the demised Atlantis Casino (formerly Playboy) and others had the darling of them all, a $2 minimum table. Las Vegas had the fun-type 25 cent table.

Regression time: Even at the $2 table we found the same imbecilic play as found in the really high-roller games.

Based on my personal experience pre-sets will tend to alter the outcome of the DICE totals in some manner conversely or inversely to the characteristics of the pre-set.

My real efforts in pre-sets began in the late 1970's in Las Vegas. This was kindergarten pre-sets.

During my infrequent trips to Atlantic City it became a process going through Junior High and High School.

Beginning with the autumn of 1991 I believe that I skipped the College of Pre-Sets and now hold umpteen degrees from various Universities of Pre-Sets.

If it works handsomely for me, it should work profitably for you.

Important: no one will ever CONTROL THE DICE outcomes.

Many will ALTER the outcomes.

PRE-SETS ARE NOT FOR PERFECTION ! ! !

BUT

PRE-SETS ARE FOR PROFITS ! ! !

There are too many variables that will work against obtaining every-time results, but over the long term profitable results will be obtained. This is worthwhile repeating. Keenly observe the other shooter's pre-sets, including the random pre-sets. Every tool in your possession to avoid the destructive final seven will assist in your profit-making. Two previous books by this author will assist earning profits.

CRAPS ILLITERACY

In the Arena of CRAP Action CRAPS illiteracy abounds. Not only is very little known about this exhilarating game, but the gambling magazines have continuous articles about this game that further mislead the public. I have tried on oh-so-many occasions to contact the "majors" in the gaming publishing world, without any success.

Telephone calls to the Win Magazine's publisher, Stan Sludikoff, exceeded ten hours. Stan, a very pleasant, knowledgeable person (other than CRAPS) at least said he disagreed with my viewpoint. Good ! At least this was a response. In time, he claims, he will get back to me — but meanwhile his magazine carried articles on CRAPS. These articles were so blazonely opposed to my thinking, that when I offered to write explanatory articles to prove my viewpoints, he said he would get back to me as soon as he further analyzed my first manuscript. In the interim, the CRAP gaming public who believe in these so-called "articles by experts" will continue to be led down to the financial sewer.

My knowledge of blackjack approaches zero. It is my opinion that the blackjack players have available good articles about their game. There were many renowned experts who really researched blackjack. The come-latelys were smart enough to only copy, modify and perhaps add a few different money management techniques. I am truly amazed that most authors on this subject state if one plays intelligently, (which would include card counting), then in the final stages before reshuffling, card counters may have a miniscule few percentage points in their favor for the remaining deck.

In order to take advantage of this situation, larger sums of money, must be placed in jeopardy's way and the cards must fall as hopefully predicted.

What do we now have ? More money at risk and the possibility that the card play will favor the larger dollar risk ! ! !

In the meantime when I review the published monthly revenue statement for the twelve Atlantic City Casinos, it is obvious that **the table game of blackjack greatly exceeds the CASINO dollar win of every other table game at every casino.**

The Casinos are laughing all the way to the bank.

In our Arena of CRAP Action, when played as suggested by this author, the **player's win percentage can be a plus instead of a minus factor.** In order to maintain a plus percentage, Zeke's Techniques must be 100% followed including the catalytic adhesive called "pre-setting DICE knowledge".

Almost every book about the game of CRAPS essentially tells you what are the best wagers in the Arena of CRAP Action. They do warn you to avoid certain wagers such as the proposition wagers and the field bets. These articles tell you to take advantage of the wagers with the minimum casino's win percentages (by maximizing - taking or laying odds) then you, the reader, could beat the casinos and win at CRAPS.

If every author states the same repetitive facts on how to win at CRAPS, then will someone please explain why less than 1% of all CRAP players are lifetime winners. This 1 % group does not include the street-smart, common-sense-wise small type players who add limited sums to their fixed incomes by avoiding the recommended pit-falls and take advantage of cycles.

I have tried on several occasions to contact Glenn Fine and Roger Gros, publisher and editor of the Casino Player. Even the Casino Player's in-house advertising contact repeatedly told me they were too busy to see me. I offered to meet with either, anytime and anywhere — but alas they were too busy. Busy or not, they ought to protect their CRAP playing readers against incorrect information.

Another additive factor for the CRAPS playing public to lose monies in the Arena of CRAP Action is the Atlantic City Magazine. Ken Weatherford is the editor. Repeatedly I tried to contact Ken Weatherford by Federal Express, faxes, telephone calls, etc. But he was too busy to discuss several of his articles on the subject of CRAPS. Though these articles were written by respected authors, they were so incorrect that it was sickening to me. One article had the "ten best casino bets" listed. I believe seven were about the game of CRAPS. In my books I prove these "seven best CRAP bets" were among the worst wagers in the game.

Upon finally contacting Ken Weatherford by telephone, he bluntly said he was too busy to see me to discuss his magazine's articles.

I did meet with Mr. John Bitzer III of the Atlantic City Magazine. He is a gentleman and listened to my disagreement with the Atlantic City Magazine's articles. Upon leaving he promised someone would contact me. I'm still waiting.

A typical gargantuan blunder these three publications have in common is when these supposedly informative (?) articles state that the more odds a pass line bettor is able to take, or the more odds a don't bettor can lay, the better these wagers become.

Every authority in CRAPS states that:

	Casino's Win Percentage
Pass Line Wager — No Odds	1.414 %
Pass Line Wager — Single Odds	0.848 %
Pass Line Wager — Double Odds	0.606 %

These casino's win percentages, as stated, are 100 % correct, but 100 % **misunderstood by EVERYONE.** The low percentages reflect the two - to - one winning ratio on the come-out-rolls.

Once the point number is established, the weighted (for all six possible point numbers) casino's win percentage is 18.79 % — *repeat 18.79 % This is the correct casino's win percentage with no odds, weighted for all six possible point numbers.*

For the various possible point numbers, at the INSTANT they are established, the casino's win percentages are:

Point Numbers	Casino's Win Percentages
4 or 10	33.33 %
5 or 9	20.00 %
6 or 8	9.09 %

This is only one of the many misunderstandings published about CRAPS in our "educational type gaming magazines".

Obviously the important objective is to publish, sell magazines and let the reader beware ! Shouldn't a magazine be responsive to its readers ? And shouldn't a magazine offer the best information available to its readers ? After all, it's a reader's privilege to disagree with what is written. But why won't they accept the proof that what they have written is wrong ?

Beware of Casino CRAPS information as presented by those who are unwilling to investigate their own articles.

BEST PRE-SET ARRANGEMENTS

Bet	Arrangement					
	A-A	B-B	C-C	A-B	A-C	B-C
		**				
Whirl Wagers on Come-out-roll	Best					
7 - 11Come-out-roll	Best					
All Six Place Bets (4, 5, 6, 8, 9, 10)					Best	
Inside Place Bets (5, 6, 8, 9)						Best
Six & Eight (6, 8)						Best
Four & Ten (4, 10)					Best	
Seven (7) Least Craps			Best			
Hardway (4, 10)				Best		
Hardways (4, 6, 8, 10)			Best			
Hi-Lo-Yo (12-2-11)	Best					
Hi-Lo (12-2)	Best					
Any Craps	Best					
Craps & Eleven	Best					
Wrong Bettor						
Least Numbers	Best					
High in Sevens	Best					
No 5 or 9	Best					

** B-B is without any "best" - just a good , normal pre-set. Good, but good for nothing in particular.

Let's take a time out to help the
WRONG BETTOR.

Not one author has ever tried to assist the wrong bettor in winning.

Before we do, let me tell the world that whenever you see a wrong bettor wagering on the Don't Pass line or making a Don't Come bet, you are watching a very stupid, unknowledgeable CRAP player

WRONG BETTOR'S ILLITERACY

When writing about CRAPS illiteracy I can't help but feel sorry for the pass line bettor's second cousin (by marriage) — the don't pass line bettor. The world of the wrong bettor reeks with craps illiteracy. How many times have you seen a sizable don't pass line bettor (or more commonly the don't come bettor) call out "No Action", when the point or new point is a 6 or 8 ? Imagine going through the deadly mine field of eight losses to three wins, and throwing away the wrong bettor's advantage of 6 to 5. No previous author ever tried to educate this type wrong bettor.

Allow me to be the first with a tremendous money making wager. Just learn to master the Pre-Set:

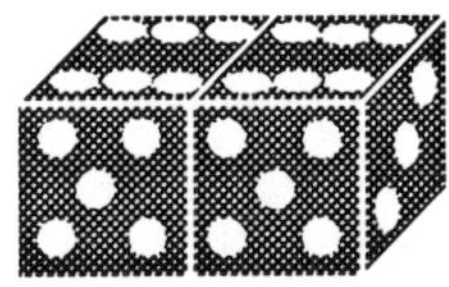

Then on the come-out-roll, or any roll, make the wagers of laying the odds against the 5, 6, 8, 9 or 4, 5, 6, 8, 9, 10. If you toss one of these numbers you only lose one wager. Protective hardway wagers (working) are superb with the 6 over 5 and 6 over 5 pre-set. Let's pass over grade-school arithmetic and go right to the bottom line. Laying $31 to $20 each on the 5 and 9 and laying $25 to $20 on each the 6 and 8 the 36 probability table theoretically results in:

18 losses totaling	=	$ 498
Wins: 6 x $80	=	$ 480
Net Loss	=	$ 18

Only one additional 7 takes the $18 loss to a win of $62 ($80 - $18). Every additional 7 creates an additional $80 profit. Naturally, if wagers are of larger magnitude, profits soar.

This is a tremendous opportunity for a pre-setter (6 over 5 and 6 over 5).

WRONG BETTOR'S WINNING PERCENTAGE

(After point number is established)

Refer to the Wrong Bettor's 1980 Probability Table.

Don't Pass Line Wins	=	784
Total Point Numbers	=	1320

$$\frac{784}{1320} = 59.39\ \%\ \text{(after point is established)}$$

Wouldn't life be sweeter if as crap players you were a wrong bettor and your exposure to risk began ONLY when the point number was established ?

There is a method that would save the wrong bettor bundles of cash equivalent chips. I call this the "Paradox of the Wrong Bettor".

Once again it must be mentioned that this vital procedure has never before been exposed by any of our non-thinking CRAP authors. Two things are necessary to accomplish disclosure. John Scarne's Wrong Bettor's 1980 Probability Table and sixth grade arithmetic.

Facts from the Wrong Bettor's 1980 Probability Table:

> On the come-out-rolls there are 440 Losers and 165 Winners. Assume our arrogant, smug, wrong bettor is wagering $20 on the Don't Pass Line (or the Don't Come). Theoretically over the course of 1980 tosses of the DICE the following analysis occurs.

Losses = 440 x $20	=	$ 8800
Wins = 165 x $20	= –	$ 3300
Net Come-Out-Roll Loss	=	$ 5500

Don't forget the theory of the 1980 Probability Table is that a wager is made 1980 times, continuously either on the Don't Pass Line or the Don't Come. There are 1320 point numbers and 660 come-out-rolls, but 55 come-out-rolls with boxcars (12) are neutral (standoff not affecting Wrong Bettor's wins or losses). Theoretically the Wrong Bettor who wagers $20 everytime is going to lose $5500 over the 605 (660 minus 55) come-out-rolls of the DICE.

Back to basics. This particular cold-shoulder type wrong bettor wanted to win $20 each time at every opportunity. What would happen if single odds were layed that the point number would evaporate in the atmosphere of 784 wrong bettor's wins accompanied with a mere 536 losses ?
The wrong bettor wants to obtain a seat on the Wrong Bettor's Stock Exchange. As a Wrong Bettor the player is in heaven once the point number is established. There are 1320 point numbers:

Pass Line Point Losers	784	784
Pass Line Point Winners	+ 536	- 536
Point Numbers	1320	
Net Pass Line Losses		248

$\frac{248}{1320} = 18.79\ \%$ Winning percentage for Wrong Bettor once point number is established.

* Object: Purchase a Seat on Wrong Bettor's Stock Exchange for LESS than $5500.

In order to obtain this most enviable position our quiet (almost always for the older high roller type) wrong bettor must lay the following:

Point Number	* Odds Layed
4 or 10	$ 41 to $ 20
5 or 9	$ 31 to $ 20
6 or 8	$ 25 to $ 20

These are the true odds plus the 5 % vigorish on the amount expected to win ($ 20).

In every instance the wrong bettor will pay 5% vigorish on the $ 20 they want to win. This arithmetically equates to $ 1 for each of the 1320 point numbers, or $1320.

Can this be ?

Boy oh boy! Is this what we think it is ? A savings of $ 4180 for our wrong betting non-confederate ? Let's analyze this together. If a $ 20 Don't Pass Line bettor were to avoid the 660 come out rolls for the 1980 tosses of the DICE, what would be saved ?

330	Losing 7's
110	Losing 11's
165	Winning Craps (2, 3)
* 55	Stand-off Boxcars (12)
660	Come-Out-Rolls
* -55	Non Decisions
605	Decisions

Net Losses = 440 - 165 = 275 for the Wrong Bettor

$20 x 275 Net Losses	=	$ 5500
Cost of 1320 Point Numbers	=	– $ 1320
Theoretical Savings	=	$ 4180

This can't be! It is too good to believe. The cost to obtain a seat on the Wrong Bettor's Stock Exchange is only $1320 for our $20 Wrong Bettor. What is the complete financial story ? Why is the seat on the Wrong Bettor's Stock Exchange so inexpensive ? After all, the seat entitles the wrong bettor to have a theoretical winning percentage of 59.39 % or almost 60 %. Wait, I hear something. The quiet wrong bettor is starting to grumble. He's thinking — aha, there is more money put in jeopardy's way. How much more money over the 1320 point numbers ?

Arithmetic time again.

Point Number	Frequency	* Odds Laid
4	165 x $ 40	$ 6,600
10	165 x $ 40	6,600
5	220 x $ 30	6,600
9	220 x $ 30	6,600
6	275 x $ 24	6,600
8	275 x $ 24	6,600
	1320	$ 39,600

Digression Time — One of the beautiful things about our perfect game of CRAPS, $ 6600 is the same for all six numbers. If we were to pay vigorish of $ 1320 for the 1320 point numbers, our additional exposure would be $ 39,600.

Normally the exposure for the 1320 point numbers would be:
1320 x $ 20 or $ 26,400.

This means our increase of exposure by laying single odds is $ 13,200. This is really too good to be true.

Additional Exposure =	$ 13,200
Savings	$ 4,180
Winning Percentage	59.39 %

THIS IS REALLY TOO GOOD TO PASS UP ! ! !

Again, I must frown with extreme dismay about the stupidity of previous authors. John Scarne laid the ground work, but alas not one previous author ever exercised good common-sense, street-sense or attempted sixth grade arithmetic.

WAIT ! ! !

We are not finished yet. The best is yet to come. Some numbers at particular times are more friendly (for the wrong bettor) than others. Once a point number is established, the Don't Pass Line Bettor or the Don't Come Bettor is locked into this point number the same way that the Pass Line Bettor is. True the don't bettor can remove his wager anytime, but only a damn stupid fool would remove the don't wager after escaping the eight losses to every three wins exposure dodging bullet after bullet on the come-out-roll. Some imbeciles do remove these wagers, primarily if the point number is the 6 or 8.

What are this author's conclusions ?

The previous exercise is being brought to the attention of the wrong bettor because if had to be done. No previous author ever attempted to assist the wrong bettor. Obviously if you want to be a wrong bettor, we have shown you the light of day. The vigorish method is not only a better procedure but the vigorish method permits the wrong bettor to lay odds against ANY PLACE BET NUMBER (or numbers).

As previously stated, some numbers are more advantageous than others, at a particular time. In my span of time at CRAP tables, it has been observed that some CRAP players periodically or consistently make notes regarding the flow of number or decisions. This is beautiful because any information is always better than no information. Even if it is partially incorrect. - BUT - when did you ever see a wrong bettor with pen and paper ?

The typical wrong bettor brings to our exhilarating CRAP Table:

(a) Better-than-thee attitude

(b) Subdued enthusiasm

(c) Larger bankroll than a typical pass line player

(d) Know-it-all attitude

(e) "Playing with the house" attitude

Let's address this last statement. Recently I glance-read a stupid gambling book on how to win. They claim over 3,000,000 copies were sold. This poor example of how to win (dice chapters) clearly stated that the best way to win was to maximize pass line and don't pass line odds. It also stated that the wrong player was playing with the house. Many wrong bettors sincerely believe they are playing with the house.

If 100 % of all CRAP players were wrong bettors, the casinos would still be a big winner — still going to the bank, everyday. Now that you have been re-educated it is time to reflect on the wrong bettor's play.

The vigorish method is the best of two bad situations.

Zeke disapproves of both the Pass Line and Don't Pass Arenas of CRAP Action.

If you want to earn profits and are willing to grind the casinos for a profit, then stay with the place bets as Zeke suggests, in the manner and techniques Zeke recommends.

PARADOX OF THE WRONG BETTOR

Let's discuss why I call this the "Paradox of the Wrong Bettor". Many wrong bettors, primarily the young or those not endorsed with inherited el dinero, will only wager a chip or two on the Don't Pass and/or Don't Come lines. These players will never lay any odds. Theoretically, a loss for this type waggering will occur 27 times over the 1925 decisions (1980 -55 for boxcars), for a casino's win percentage of 1.40259%.

The wrong bettor thereotically would lose 27 times the dollar amount of the Don't wager over the 1980 loss. The Don't player we exampled who wagered $20 would theoretically lose 27 x $ 20 or a total of $ 540. Paying 5 % vigorish for the privilege of attempting to win $ 20 each time, the cost of vigorish is 1320 times $ 1 or a total of $ 1320. This is $ 780 more than the projected $ 540 Don't bettor's loss.

Think about it ! What we have is the ***"Paradox for the Wrong Bettor".***

It really does not matter. Wrong bettor, and Right bettor, are both horrendous wagers.

Allow me to offer a cutesy pre-set betting play for a pre-setter. Sometimes, but not to often, when I am pre-setting and obtaining an abnormally high rate of 7's on the come out roll (and it happens more frequently than not), I will lay $ 112 to $ 80 that no inside numbers (5, 6, 8, 9) will appear on the come out roll.

This is one good thing I will say for a Wrong bettor. If an inside number is generated on the come-out-roll then depending upon the point number, either $30 or $24 is lost (plus $1 vigorish). Then the remaining three numbers are removed with the RETURN of the $1 vigorish.

As a Right betting place bettor, when a 7 is generated ***all*** the walls of Jericho's Place come tumbling down. This is the only thing I like about Wrong betting - ***only one pillar*** of Jericho's wall comes down from the force of one fatal toss of the dice.

WINNING

Pre-Setting by itself is insufficient to create profits.

Understanding the Arena of CRAP Action is a must. Knowing where to place your wagers is very important as is when to remove, increase, or decrease them. The three methods of charting are fundamental and the very best tool for winning.

Respecting those ominous sevens should be like going to your Hippodrome of Worship. One should know oneself, and be patient, self-disciplined and not greedy.

Then take a deep breath and relax. The Arena of CRAP Action should be fun, pressure free along with the anticipation of the exhilarating stickman's call.

HORN WAGER - DEFINED AND REDESIGNED

A horn wager is a one roll wager. It is simply an easy way to state that you want to wager one unit each on the 2, 3, 11 and 12. The unit can be anything from $ 1 to the limit allowed. Some casinos allow a maximum pay-off of $ 15,000. This means the most a wager could be on snake-eyes (1 - 1) or boxcars (6 - 6) would be $ 500. There are six ways to make (win) a horn wager. This author's preference is the *whirl wager* which includes the 7 having a unit wager. With the pre-set the stickperson's call "Seven" keeps the five unit wager alive for the next roll as the payoff for the seven is 4 to 1. Normally the "any red" wager is a stupid wager giving the casino a 16.67 % win percentage.

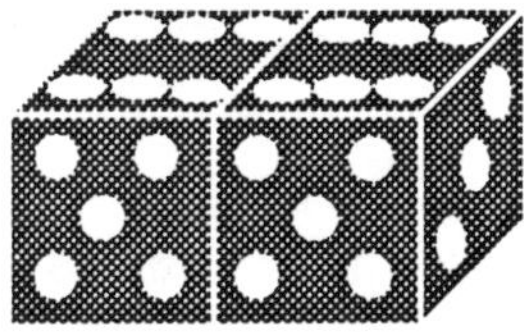

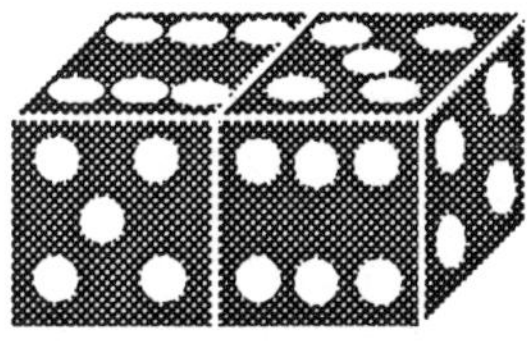

This author's pre-sets: permits this author to win more often on the pass line on the come-out-roll and allows the whirl wager to stay alive for another toss of our dice.
Both these pre-sets on the come-out-roll are superb profit makers. The hardways's working on the come-out-roll with a protective wager on the 7 is definitely a profit maker for me. After changing my pre-set once the point number is established, sometimes intuitively, I may say, "Hardway wagers are now a horn wager". Depending on the point number, an additional unit wager will be tossed to the stickperson.

ZEKE'S PRE-SET IDIOSYNCRASIES

Zeke always pre-sets the DICE. There are various pre-sets for different financial goals. Many times in the middle of a roll, different pre-sets may be selected to attempt altering the frequency of certain place bet numbers or a group of numbers (whirls, hardways, etc.) After a place bet number is hit (won) changes are ***Always made ! ! !*** Never a dormant **"Same bet"**. Place bets will be removed completely or partially removed depending upon the glance interpretation of the chart.

When the place bet wagers are larger than normal, some wagers may be decreased or removed.

NEVER does Zeke press the place bets ! ! !

If the stickperson presents the dice with the Hardway four on top (2 - 2) then I will lightly toss the dice against the wall beneath to obtain a different total for the top surfaces. This is a definitive ritual when the A - C arrangement of 1 over two and two over three.

Should the stickperon's dice format show the acey-deuce (1 - 2) on top, I will adjust the dice so that die with the one on top will be pre-set with the two dots on the top over the front surface of three dots. The second die will be changed to one dot on top and the front surface will have two dots. This is strictly a superstitious shtick. No rationale whatsoever. Just one of my kiddy-kicks.

It will be the practice of 99% of all stickpersons NOT to present the shooter with any crap numbers on the top surfaces, but the many stickpersons who know my play will place the dice before me with any top surface totals EXCEPT the 7. I will accept double numbers on the top surfaces, a few shooters will not.

NEVER do I ADD a place bet wager once the original place bet wagers are made. Quite a number of players will either PRESS a place bet wager or ADD a place bet number, if one is hit. Sometimes they will do both simultaneously, add a place bet wager and press another place bet wager. This procedure is strictly forbidden in our place bet wagering format.

Another of my idiosyncrasies is removing the place bets if a co-player blurts, "this is a great roll, keep it up." Jinxes work to my advantage, as the deadly seven is soon on the scene.

When wagering on the inside four numbers (5, 6, 8, 9) and one is hit (won), I never leave the 5 and 9 alive ALONE. At least one of the six's and eight's must remain with the 5 and 9. But this condition is a very rare exception. Never do I permit the chart to indicate ONLY the 5 and 9 as my last two remaining place bet wagers.

My favorite preset

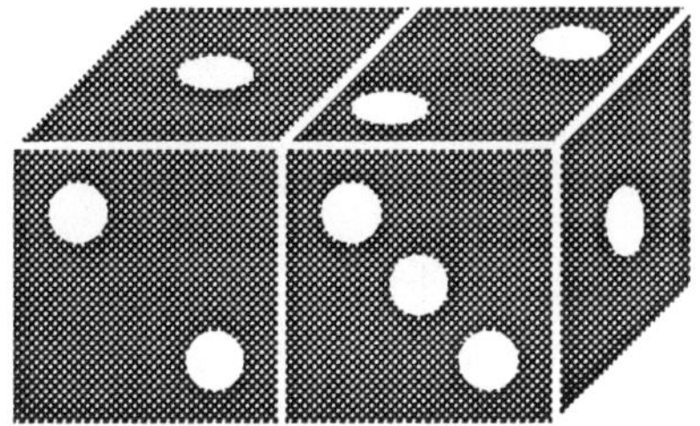

permits me to attempt the 4 and 10 when chart approved with the hardways 4 and 10. One of the oddities of this pre-set is for the hardways 6 and 8 to appear more frequently than theoretically expected.

CASINO CRAPS IS A VICIOUS GAME

The casino's win percentage as represented by the New Jersey Casino Commission is approximately fifteen (15 %).

This fifteen (15 %) casino's win percentage is based on actual gross amount of cash and markers exchanged for gambling chips. The net amount of actual money exposed to the exciting, exhilarating game of craps is substantially less. (See article in this book about "Casinos Devour Over 34 % of the CRAP Bankroll"). This we will call the 'true drop'.

According to a fourteen month study by this author, the actual casino's win percentage of true drop exceeds 34 %.

WHY ?

The answer became obvious when I decided to study the *Game Of Casino Craps.*

Every author who has ever written about this fantastic exciting game recommends the identical methods to "win at Casino CRAPS".

They all repeat the identical garbage. If all these authors agree on how to win at Casino CRAPS, then someone ought to explain why less than 1 % of Casino Craps players are overall winners.

The late John Scarne was the very best author and expert on all phases of gambling. His books, especially on DICE, inspired me to further investigate the game of CRAPS. Personally, I treasure his superb books on all types of gambling.

Okay, if you are satisfied to grind for **profit,** we can now proceed.

These methods can be applied to any size wagers to reap profits.

I like to consider my techniques as *not gambling,* but more like *grinding the Casinos* for profit.

This author is the only CRAP author to state ***"The only way to win at casino Craps is through the *green pastures of the Place bets".***

As of this writing no one has developed a system or technique to win overall in the Arena of CRAP action. No one has put forth a workable money management system to win overall in Casino CRAPS.

That is why approximately five to eight out of a thousand CRAP players are overall winners. *This is less than 1 %.*

This means, that as of April 1992, there were 214 CRAP tables in the twelve Atlantic City Casinos. Most of these CRAP tables hold 12 *potential losers.* The fewer large CRAP tables allow 16 *almost non-existent winners* to participate in the exciting Palladium of CRAP Action.

Less than 2700 CRAP players are needed to have 100 % capacity at any one given moment. Of these 2700 potential victims of those dazzlin' DICE, only 81, or 3 %, would leave the casinos as winners. This equates to 97 % of the players lose their bankroll because they are uneducated in the Arena of CRAP Action. As these same 81 players play another day, or later sessions during the year, the overall winners will dwindle

* As in Green Dollar Signs.

to about 24 from the original 2700. This is less than 1 % of our theoretical 2700.

The Hippodrome of Casino CRAPS is a dying gambling game. This is evidenced by the fact that before Donald Trump's Taj Mahal, the total number of CRAP tables in Atlantic City approached 250. The Taj Mahal added 30 more CRAP tables,

BUT

the total has dwindled to only 214 at years end. The Bally Grand and others are removing CRAP tables to make room for additional slot machines. As of June 1, 1992, the total number of CRAP Tables dwindled to 187 in Atlantic City's twelve casinos.

In Las Vegas most casinos have few CRAP tables. Steve Wynn's Mirage has 12 CRAP tables. Caesar's Palace has 13 CRAP tables. Many others have only one, two or three.

There are two reasons why this exhilarating game of CRAPS shows declining trends.

First Reason:

> A miniscule percentage of casino personnel and CRAP players really understand Casino CRAPS. This equates to less than 1 % of the Casino personnel able to give you a correct answer to specific question on the finer points of CRAPS.

Second Reason:

Casino CRAPS is a very fast, confusing game. Old timers learned CRAPS in the streets and in the armed services. The younger generation cannot cope with the variety of wagers and the speed of the game. No one can cope with the Casino CRAP'S appetite for devouring over 34 % of the players bankroll.

In a recent poll that I supervised, I asked 316 *Casino personnel two basic questions:

(a) What is the best wager in the Arena of CRAP Action ?
(b) Is it better to "buy" the place bets 4 or 10, or merely place bet the 4 or 10 if you intend pressing (increasing) these wagers when they become winners ?

Poll Results for (a) :

Pass Line Bet with Maximum Odds	87
Don't Pass Line Bet with Maximum Odds	229
**Total Idiots	316

Poll Results for (b) :

"Buy" the 4 or 10	316
Place bet the 4 or 10	0
**Total Imbeciles	316

* Dealers, Floor Supervisors, Pit Managers, Shift Managers and top very highly paid Casino Executives.

** These totals have more than doubled since my first book Articles in this book will clearly explain that both the Pass

Line and Don't Pass Line are **poor wagers.** The supposedly "true odds" is a trap for further transforming these **poor wagers** into **disastrous wagers.**

Every other CRAP *auth*or (as in *auth*ority) stupidly claims the Pass Line and Don't Pass Line wagers are the very best in the Arena of CRAP action. They also state these wagers improve as you take or lay maximum odds. After reading the article in "Decreasing Percentages" you will understand why copy-cat authors are not the authority.

When making wagers on the Place bets 4 or 10 it is better to "buy" the first wager. To "buy" the 4 or 10 the player pays the casino a commission of 5% to obtain the true odds of 2 to 1, instead of 9 to 5. This is called vigorish in the Arena of CRAP action. The advantage on the first buy is less than 5% over Place betting the 4 or 10. After the very first win, the win factor increases dramatically in favor of Place betting the four or ten. As an example, compare the difference between "buying" the 4 or 10 and Place betting the 4 or 10. If a player is fortunate to overcome the odds of 728 to 1 for six fully pressed "buy" bets, compared to fully pressing the place bets, the advantage for the place bettor is 12.89 times greater than the "buy" bettor. Repeat: after beating the odds of 728 to 1 for winning six times on the 4 or 10, the financial return (per dollar invested) is thirteen times better for the Place bettor. This is thirteen hundred percent (1300 %) better. Every additional win further expands the Place bettor's advantage.

Not one person in the Arena of CRAP Action ever disclosed this fact. No one, not the authors, the experts or casino people even knew this fact.

Warning - this author *does not approve* of the 4 or 10 Place bets unless charting indicates a very rare wager is viable.

Repeat: CRAP Authors and Casino Personnel comprise the know-nothing-ism of the CRAPS society.

WHAT HAPPENS TO PLAYER'S CRAP BANKROLL ?

* Typical CRAP Session

Percentage of CRAP bankroll *lost*	Percentage of Players
100 %	27 %
50 %	35 %
20 %	16 %
10 %	11 %
0 % (Breakeven)	8 %
** Winners	3 %
	100 %

Percentages were obtained over a period of 24 months by periodically asking various players what the final financial results were the last session they played Casino CRAPS. By session it is meant the total time a CRAP player spent during a particular visit to the Atlantic City casinos. In some cases, it was a weekend, a doy or so, others varied from a few hours, four to six hours or in the case of novices, perhaps 15 to 40 minutes.

* Author's opinion. Please note that these percentages are not related to dollars loss.

** These are winners for a particular session.

Overall winners, during the course of time, *dwindle to less than one percent of all CRAP players.*

THE CRAP PLAYER'S *UNKNOWN CURSE*

If you heard it once, you heard it hundreds of times.

> **"Dice have no memory and every toss or roll of the dice is completely independent of any previous toss of the dice."**

This is the ***curse*** of all CRAP players.

* Because of this curse *all* crap players have *lost* quite a bundle of chips !

* Whenever CRAP players approach a table in the middle of an unknown roll and make sizeable wagers they will be **doomed.**

WAIT

**Another Friend Is Going
To Enhance Our
Chances Of Earning
Profits**

CHARTING

This is the most important singular chapter of this book ! ! !

EVASION, YES AVOIDANCE

In order to be in a posture to win you will need all the tools available. Our attack on Casino CRAPS is actually an evasion *not an invasion.* Sounds contradictory !

A better choice of etymology would be *avoidance.*

Yes, avoidance.

This book will *not* assist you in playing CRAPS as it is **improperly played** in today's 'Arena of CRAP Action'. That's why there are over 99 % losers ! ! !

Forget any information you may have read or heard about the Game of CRAPS.

Our approach will be to find various methods, techniques and superstitions to avoid the 7's. This will minimize the appearance of those financially destructive 7's.

You will never eradicate the 7's. All you want to accomplish is simply to obtain **four Place bet wins for ever singular losing 7.** Therefore our goal will be to avoid some of those critical 7's.

Besides being the most important chapter of this book, *CHARTING* is also the most prolific. Prior to re-writing the introduction to charting, 79 type-written pages on this subject were compiled plus an additional 40 odd handwritten pages.

Let's begin

Charting is compiling the flow of DICE numbers generated as the various shooters toss the DICE against the furthest padded wall.

Recall the CRAP Player's CURSE:

"Dice have no memory and every toss or roll of the dice is completely independent of any previous toss of the dice."

If the CRAP players curse is correct, can the compiling the flow of past numbers assist us in projecting future outcomes ?

YES !

YES ! !

OH MY, YES ! ! !

CAN CHARTING REALLY HELP ?

How can previous charting be of any assistance ? This is a very fair and valid question.

If we were able to chart the CRAP action generated numbers for all the CARP tables in the world for the next five or ten years, or go back in time and recapture the charting of all Las Vegas CRAP action for one day or 10 years, we would be amazed at the similarity of the charts.

These charts would include many of those once-in-a-lifetime so called *hot streaks.*

They would also include too many of those heart-breaking cold streaks (for the right bettors).

What does the charting REVEAL ?

By compiling the series of numbers generated by those intriguing DICE, certain predictions can be made. This will *minimize our loss periods* and ***maximize our profit periods.***

This procedure is called CHARTING. Charting is accomplished by observing live CRAP action at the casinos. It also can be obtained by randomizing CRAP numbers on computers, or compiling numbers in the CRAP game called Pass Line Craps.

CHART READING

Chart reading is meant to be only '*glance read*'. **There is no need to study your chart.**

Just by 'glancing' at the chart you will gather sufficient information to act accordingly. A glance reader is as effective, as if the rolls generated were to be used as input to a high-tech computer. In this case, however, the computer is your brain.

NO COMPUTER CAN ACCURATELY PREDICT WHAT THE NEXT NUMBER OR NUMBERS GENERATED WILL BE TOSSED BY THE SHOOTER.

Your glance reading will give you a *good intuitive feeling* for the future outcome.

There will be *failures*, but the *successes* will greatly outnumber the failures, by at least a 4 to 1 ratio.

Once it's realized that shorter rolls greatly exceed the longer rolls, then you are on the way to profitable playing.

PROFITS

WITH

PLEASURE

It will be best to chart, Super-chart and Mega-chart, and you must chart to earn consistent profits.

Charting is to compile the continuous flow of numbers generated by everyone.

Super-charting is maintaining a running total of Sevens (7's) as compared to ***all the numbers.*** Theoretically, one-sixth of all the numbers generated will be a Seven (7).

Mega-charting is keeping a running total ***of the inside numbers (5, 6, 8, 9)*** and comparing this with the running total of all numbers. Theoretically, one-half of all the numbers created by the DICE will be inside numbers (5, 6, 8, 9).

The principle attached to all phases of charting is that "in time" everything should be what is expected, as per the 36 Probability Table.

During fifteen years of charting, it is clear that within a reasonable time (up to two hours) these numbers have a pattern. They are askew, either above or below what the probability table predicts. Then they are in "tune" as per the probability table. Once they are on "target" as predicted, the inevitable occurs - they are askew again, or out of balance. This is an ongoing situation: On target - out of balance - on target - out of balance, etc.

Ninety-five (95 %) percent of the time this will occur within a reasonable time. The other five (5 %) percent of the time the erratic numbers go off in a tangent. The onslaught of too many 7's make the chart appear erotic or even erosive.

By coping intelligently with the 95 % element of time, earnings can be consistently maintained,

BUT

even during the other 5 % time element, earnings can be maintained, but at a much slower pace ! ! !

Even at a very, very ice cold table *earnings can be maintained if your charting is properly interpreted.* It can be done. It is being done. No one else at the table is smiling (right bettors), because no one else at the table is charting.

We must take a disadvantage in life and turn it into an advantage. Charting will do this — exchange an erratic flow of numbers into profits.

Look at your various charts, before you delve into the financially crunching world of CRAPS.

Analyze your charts when playing. If you are going to succeed you must have

PATIENCE,
DISCIPLINE,
LACK OF GREED

and a bit of intelligence- not mathematical or scientific - just plain ole' common sense and street sense.

The ocean of CRAPS is yours to swim, wade or drown ! ! !
Think - but use your head.

Above all don't be greedy. Be disciplined ! ! !

In addition to Patience, Discipline and Lack of Greed, you, as a potential provider of profits, must add that all important blending ingredient:

INTUITION

SUPER-CHARTING 7's

Super-Charting is compiling on an ongoing basis the number of 7's generated by those excitable DICE, in comparison to the total numbers generated.

Chapters can be written on the importance of super-charting 7's. Over the long period of time the total number of 7's will be approximately one-sixth of all the numbers generated by the DICE. For the short term DICE created numbers are chaotic, erratic and even erotic.

It is with the present action that we are concerned. Sometimes the 7's are on target equaling one-sixth of the total numbers. Other times there are too many sevens, primarily at the wrong time for right bettors. Rarely are the 7's scarce.

By watching the ratio of 7's as compared to the total numbers we can ***increase*** our profits.

A most important result of observing the 7's has permitted this author to leave a "warm" table that is about to turn "cold." Losers try to find "hot" tables or "hot" rolls to recapture part of their losses. I leave profit making tables that are primed to turn "cold" to seek the more available "normal" CRAP tables.

Profits are best obtained at "normal" tables, less likely at "hot" tables when using Zeke's techniques. This is obvious because if one or two place bet wins is our goal per shooter, we are out in left field if a shooter has five, eight, ten or more inside place bet numbers numbers. I care less.Read articles later in this book that PROVE two wins are more profitable than five inside place bet wins.

The best part of super-charting combined with mega-charting is that **PROFITS** continue on what losers call "cold" tables.

Basically profits increase at a faster rate on "normal" tables and "cold" tables. The rare "hot" rolls and "hot" tables leave me as a spectator after the quota of one or two Place Bet wins. I am leery of these tepid conditions because of the equilibrium principle.

The best tool available to act as a catalyst for super-charting is your own intuition.

Let the perpetual losers seek out the long rolls or "hot" table. I'll take the "normal" or even "cold" tables for profiteering.

Lead not your wagers into temptation.

Glance read the charts.

Don't be Greedy, have patience.

MEGA-CHARTING

Mega-Charting takes a few seconds per shooter's roll. It is simply maintaining a running total of the inside (5, 6, 8, 9) numbers. There are eighteen ways to make these inside numbers, or *ONE-HALF* of the 36 numbers possible.

Glance reading the ongoing running total and comparing this total to the total numbers generated gives you an excellent feeling on how and when to wager, or increase or decrease wagers.

Mega-Charting only succeeds when guided by the super-charting. If a normal rate of 7's (one-sixth ratio) **exists** then the ratio of the inside numbers (5, 6, 8, 9) is the prevailing factor. If the inside numbers is less than one half, loosen ye' wallets. When the ratio is abnormally higher than one-half and the 7's are normal or less than one-sixth, thread lightly. This is fun time, because your intuition is an additional guiding force. The over-riding factor is always the ratio of the 7's.

The inside numbers (5, 6, 8, 9) radio only comes into play when the 7's ration are normal or higher than normal.

THE CRITICAL DECISION MAKER FOR MEGA-CHARTING IS THE VALUES OF 7's.

THE HIGHER THE RATIO OF 7's ABOVE ONE-SIXTH AVERAGE, THE BETTER THE OPPORTUNITY FOR EARNING PROFITS.

These are exceptions when the inside numbers ratio is exceptionally LESS than one-half. In defiance of the 7's ratio, I exploit the situation for additional wins. So can you. Let your own intuition be your guide to success. Be careful not to allow your intuition instincts to be overworked, or "burnt out."

CHARTING PAD FORMAT

Casino Taj Mahal Date 5-20 Start 2:10 End

L	W	1	2	3	4	5	6	7	8	9	10	11	12	13	14	15	16	17	Inside #	7's	Total #
L		(8)	3	2	6	9	7												3	1	6
L		7	(9)	5	10	10	8_H	7_{OT}											6	3	13
L		(4)	11	7															–	4	16
	W	12	(6)	8	6														9	–	20
L		(5)	3	9	3	7_{NS}													11	5	25
L		(10)	8	5	7														13	6	29
	W	11	(5)	4	5														15	–	33
	W	(9)	5	9															18	–	36

Designations:

(9) Circled number is point number

OT Off Table

H Hardways 4, 6, 8 & 10

CS Corner Shooter

NS New Stickperson

PS Pre-Set Shooter

DD Dropped DIE or DICE

A pre-printed 4" x 6" charting pad that has provisions for charting, super-charting and mega-charting is available. This easy to use pad also contains Zeke's techniques and charting samples.

Contact:
Hi-Lo-Yo Publishing Company
P.O. Box 3066
Margate, NJ 08402-3066

CASINOS DEVOUR OVER 34 % OF CRAP BANKROLL

MISTAKEN IDENTIFICATION

The New Jersey Casino Commission together with all Atlantic City Casinos unwittingly erred in calculating the true Casino's win percentage for CRAPS,

The data obtained by the drop and win figures gives the commission a basis for reference. However, I state that the Casino's real win percentage is higher than published.

By simple arithmetic, we can show that there is a "duplication" of dollar drop. The Casino's dollar win divided by a lower correct dollar drop would result in a higher Casino win percentage in CRAPS.

Let's think about this for a moment.

Assume that a typical player exchanges $200 for chips. After playing CRAPS for two hours, lets suppose it may be time for lunch or dinner. The run-of-the-mill player goes to the cashier's cage and exchanges the chips for $80 or $280 in currency depending on whether he was ahead or behind. Why carry around dirty, heavy chips when temporarily leaving the casino ?

After eating something light, the player returns to the CRAP Action Arena and exchanges possibly $100 or $200 for chips. Now what do we have ? If the player never exchanged chips for currency until the very end of play, be it at the end of one session, one day, one weekend, or as long as he or she is a player — then the dollar drop would be lower. Think about it !

Sometimes players will cash-in their chips to change their luck.

I am certain that you as a reader can offer more times when chips are exchanged for currency:

Security Reasons	Massage Time
Snack Time	Rest Periods
Fitness Room Visits	Show Time
Swim Time	etc.

After talking with key casino executives, I find that it is a practice among some players with higher credit limits to ask for a sizable marker, possibly play for a short period of time and then leave the casino. In this manner the player has obtained an interest free loan.

One of the casinos top credit executives told me of a prominent Atlantic City businessman who obtained a marker for $25,000. Then proceeding immediately to the cashier's cage to cash-in. Thus easily securing an interest free "loan".

Apparently this is more common that I expected. I also was informed that many players frequently cash in their chips for fresh money. They hope to give the impression to the casino people that they are investing more money so they can obtain larger comps. These two examples certainly add to the false dollar drop figures, and according to top knowledgeable executives, the dollar drop is dramatically affected by these false dollar drops.

Information obtained from casino executives was encouraging. One source estimated this duplication at about 30 %. Six other sources stated it ranged from 20 % to 25 %. These estimates were in the proper direction, but low ! ! !

NEW JERSEY CASINO CONTROL COMMISSION RESULTS

1991 Recorded CRAPS Drop	=	$ 2,275,571,000
Casino's Dollar Win	=	$ 348,872,000
Casino's Win Percentage	=	15.33 %

AUTHOR'S EVALUATION

The average typical CRAP player's time would be one daily session.

During a four months period, I spoke to over four hundred players. These conversations took less than two minutes each. The following analysis was predicated on a typical 100 CRAP players.

Question:

> "Normally how many times during a day do you cash in your chips for any reason such as meal time showtime or breaktime ?"

Analysis:

Players	Extra trip to Cash In	False Drops
34	0	0
27	1	27
21	2	42
14	3	42
3	4	12
1	5	5
100		128

Let's assume, for simplicity, that these 100 typical CRAP players initially purchased $100 in chips. Now a break is needed. It may be that he or she may be down $30 to $40 or up possibly $20 to $80. It really does not matter. If player A is down $27 and received $73 for his or her chips, it is almost a certainty that upon returning to the casino another $100 bill will be tendered for chips. If player B won $61 and received $161 for the chips, it is again a certainty that he will also tender $100 for chips when re-entering the Arena of CRAP Action.

CRAP TABLE

Dealer
Boxperson
Stickperson
Dealer
PASS LINE
NO CALL BETS
Don't Pass Bar
Don't Come Bar
PLACE BETS
4
5
SIX
8
NINE
10
COME
2 3 · 4 · 9 · 10 · 11 12
FIELD
Pays Double
BIG 6 8
HARDWAYS
9 TO 1
7 TO 1
ONE ROLL BETS
ANY SEVEN 4 TO 1
30 TO 1
15 TO 1
HORN BET
ANY CRAPS 7 TO 1
C E

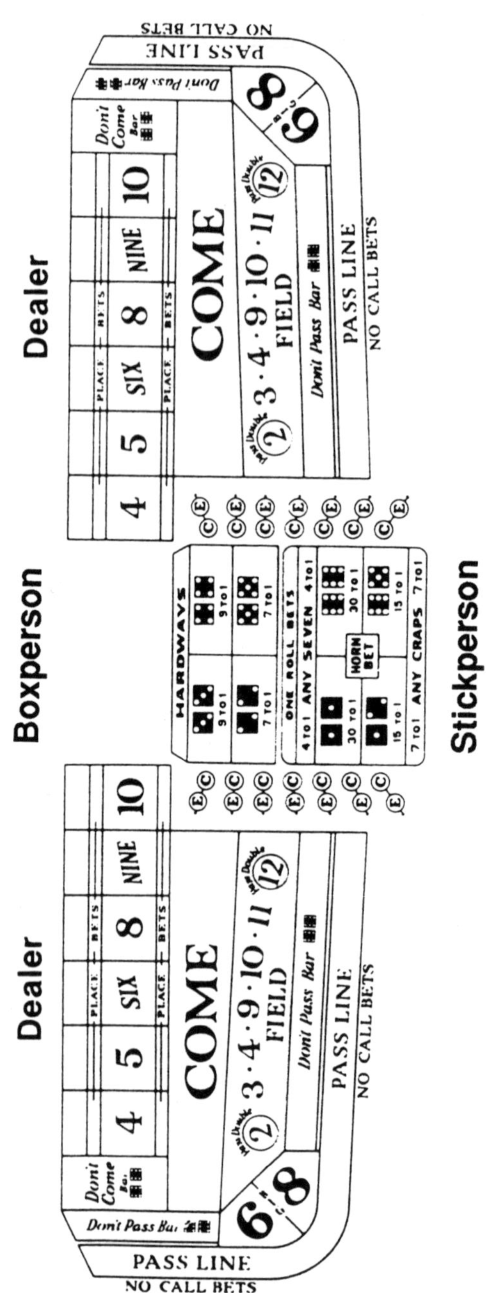

ZEKE'S TECHNIQUES

1. For earning PROFITS *only* wager on the place bets.

2. ***Never press Place bets***

3. Best bet would be one hit (win) and complete removal of all place bets, preferably the inside numbers of 5, 6, 8 and 9. Then wait for new shooter for next wager.

4. Add insurance factor by charting.

5. Add additional insurance by super-charting. Super-charting is the compiling and comparing the total number of 7's to the total numbers rolled (including 7's). Theoretically, the 7's should be one-sixth of the total numbers.

6. Mega-charting adds an important flavor of insurance. Mega-charting is keeping a running total of inside numbers (5, 6, 8, 9) as compared to total numbers generated. Mega-charting is only effective when Super-charting indicates that future rolls could be low in 7's. Inside numbers (5, 6, 8, 9) theoretically should be one-half of total numbers.

7. Increase value of place bets only after win at beginning of new shooter, when suggested by Chart, Super-chart and Mega-chart.

8. **Never play Pass Line unless shooting DICE.** When shooting

(as in fun time, etc.) place at least three place bets. If equipped with proper pre-set, then possibly go for two or more wins.

9. Avoid proposition bets except for fun time, pre-set time and intuitive time.

10. Five place bets when chart approved are superb bets. Be careful about second or more wins. Suggest removal of first hit place bet, then remove each successive win. If removed bets are generated again then remove balance of place bets. Financial risk is greater than normal, be very very careful. Only place five wagers when ahead ! ! !

11. Historical charting shows that if place bet is not won within a given number of tosses, it is wise to remove all place bets. This given number can range from five to seven depending upon charting and intuitive feeling. Given numbers include every number from beginning of roll, including numbers before establishing point number.

12. There is no scientific reason for this, but if first three numbers of new shooter are craps, sevens or elevens (any combination) this author has gained by not making any Place bets. My personal records for the past 15 years indicate that the odds against any point number being made exceeds 5 to 1. Now you know this should not be the case, but for me it works.

13. Omitted for superstitious reasons.

14. Place bets on all six numbers (4, 5, 6, 8, 9 AND 10) are

superior bets for one, two, and three possible hits when chart approved. Suggest removal of place bets that are won. If removed place bet is hit again, then remove remaining place bets. Intuition and charting should help in decision. **Very risky, even for the experienced player.** It is preferred to opt for two wins on the four inside numbers (5, 6, 8, 9).

15. When place bets have higher dollar value than your normal wager and you are attempting a second win, **it is strongly suggested** that you reduce dollar amount for second attempt. Also remove place bet that is won, or at least reduce dollar value on winning place bet.

16. **Remove all Place wagers if any of the following occurs:**

    (1) One or both dice leave the CRAP table.
    (2) The shooter drops one DIE or both DICE.
    (3) A new stickperson replaces the previous stickperson.
    (4) The shooter throws the DICE nonchalantly with no sincerity.
    (5) The shooter changes one or both DICE.
    (6) The shooter whips DICE with much more than normal force against back wall.
    (7) Shooter aims for either corner of back wall.
    (8) Any time that player feels intuitively that the ugly seven is due.

17. Pass Line betting time.
    (a) Fun Time
    (b) Superstitious Time
    (c) Intuitive Time

18. **Never** chase a consecutive series of shooter's losing rolls without any inside numbers (5, 6, 8 and 9) appearing before the ugly seven, after new point number is established. This inside **number (5, 6, 8, or 9) must**appear within three additional tosses after establishing point number.

19. **Never** increase Place bets after a loss.

20. **Never** make Place bets in the middle of an unknown roll.

21. When properly increasing dollar value of place bets, chart and intuition may suggest increasing certain place bets selectively above basic increase. Definitely when any of these numbers are hit and won, remove this number completely and again reduce dollar value of other place bets. Sometimes I benefit leaving wagers on the 6 AND 8, no matter if one of these was hit already.

22. **Never** work Place bets on the come out roll.

23. **Never** wager on the family of Don't Pass Bets and Don't Come Bets.

24. **Never** wager on the family of Pass Line Bets and Come Bets. When you are a shooter, play Pass Line but ***no*** Come bets. Taking odds is a preference of Pre-set and intuition. (Six months later, after comfortably earning an income).

25. An excellent technique when playing the inside place bets on the 5, 6, 8 and 9; if 5 or 9 is made (won) then remove both the 5 & 9 and let the 6 & 8 remain. If the 6 **or** 8 is hit then remove **both** the 6 and 8. **IMPORTANT:** If 5 or 9 is repeated again, remove **both** the 6 and 8.

26. **Avoid** Place bets on the 4 or 10. Even when chart approved and good intuitive feeling, it is a gamble - a very low percentage of earning any income.

VERY IMPORTANT:

Whenever you approach ANY CRAP TABLE, chart and observe the numbers generated by the DICE for at least 10 minutes. This would be a minimum of 22 numbers.

HORRENDOUS WAGERS ! ! !

• Pass Line
• Don't Pass Line
• Come Bet
• Don't Come Bet
• Vigorish to Buy 4 or 10
• Place Bets 4 or 10
• Odds Behind Pass Line
• Laying Odds for Wrong Bettor
• Pressing Any Place Bets

The above imbecilic stupid CRAP play accounts for over 92 % of the casino's dollar win at CRAPS.

Casino CRAPS cannot be BEAT as suggested by *other authors, so called crap experts* or *gambling authorities.*

Please explain to me why there are less than one percent overall CRAP winners. Could it be because every book written on how to win at CRAPS or Beat the Casino repeats the same smelly garbage? Some attempt cute-sy plays, and others try money management. When, in the final analysis the success rate winning at CRAPS is less than one percent. And these winners did not learn anything from the "experts". They combined street-sense with common sense to become self-taught.

You should be angry, embittered and disgusted that you followed the CRAP cowpath of previous players and authors. A winning success rate of only one percent (and those were probably SELF-TAUGHT) suggested *pit-falls* with other playing methods.

I am also irritated. Education, in any subject matter, should enable you to go further in life to newer heights — *not* directing you to the FINANCIAL SEWER ! ! !

Today, the success rate for winners in the Arena of CRAP Action is LESS than one (1%) percent.

The success rate of my readers should greatly exceed twenty (20 %) percent. This rate is more than twenty times greater than present day winners.

Failures will result *not* because of the call of the wild (stickman's call), but because people are basically *greedy*. They want one more place bet win, sometimes after a full press. Or they *lack patience*. Combined, these faults will exist because of *no self discipline*.

This twenty-plus percent success rate could be much higher. High enough to force the luxurious casinos to change CRAP odds in order to continue making a profit in the Hippodrome of CRAP Action.

The rate of CRAP success will not increase because of human nature:

GREED

LACK OF PATIENCE

LACK OF DISCIPLINE

Even those that fail will recognize it was not because of the call of the wild (stickman's call of the DICE numbers generated). Honest thinking losers will admittedly blame themselves in disgust. Some will retrench and go back to basics, most will not ! ! !

THIS IS WHY PLACE BETTORS ARE LOSERS !

Two Wins Are More Profitable Than Five Wins
Two Wins Are Better Than Six Wins

This is very intriguing. There is a mathematical basis for making such a statement. Let's first assume using the four inside numbers (5, 6, 8, 9), each with the minimum wager ($22 total), we have been on target chart-wise and have recorded two wins so far. At the point of the second win, the profit for this shooter is two times $7 or $14.

If we now remove our four inside wagers, our $14 profit for this shooter is clearly protected. Let's project into the future what would happen if we permitted our $22 investment to remain as we go for broke:

Win #	Profit Including This Win	Net Income if 7 Before next Win
3	$ 21	Loss $ 1
4	$ 28	Profit $ 6
5	$ 35	Profit $ 13
6	$ 42	Profit $ 20

This projection should help us take a positive posture. The most serious decision a CRAP player has when he is pressing his place bets is *when should he completely remove or decrease dollar value of Press Bets.* This is really a dilemma ! !

Let's relate this to the fortunate profiteer who has two wins for a $14 profit if the inside (5, 6, 8, 9) place bets are removed.

This is clearly the only decision our income earner can make if the goal is to become a consistent winner.

Be content with two wins, a profit of $14. If greedy for the elusive long inside number rich roll, after three additional wins on the inside numbers (5, 6, 8, 9) and then a loss of $22, the profit would have decreased to $13. Going for four additional wins profit will increase from $14 to $20 if a destructive seven then appears.

I repeat - going for three additional wins (total of five) and then the 7's pops up. This reduces the $14 profit to $13.

Four additional wins, and then a non-removal of place bets, results in a total profit for this shooter of $20 when the 7 appears.

Good gosh ! Five wins for less profit than two wins ($13 instead of $14).

Gosh by golly ! Six total wins (or four wins more than two wins) increases profits from $14 to $20. But you must travel through hell avoiding 7's for four additional wins for a mere increase of only $6.

You make this simple decision. Same dilemma as the Place Bet Presser. ***When do you remove the place bets or decrease risk ?***

My solution: Go easy. The casino wants you to give them time with the action so they can tempt you with comps. These comps will grind you down and out. Obviously you want to grind the Casino for your just reward.

This analysis is very basic and simple. Never before disclosed or discussed by any previous author. It is just an added event why there are less than 1 % overall winners in the exhilarating Hippodrome of CRAP Action.

WHEN PLACE BETTING ALL SIX NUMBERS

TWO WINS ARE MORE PROFITABLE THAN SIX WINS

AND BETTER THAN SEVEN WINS

Win #	Profit Including This Win	Net Income if 7 Before next Win
1	$ 7.50	Loss $ 24.50
2	$ 15.00	Loss $ 17.00
3	$ 22.50	Loss $ 9.50
4	$ 30.00	Loss $ 2.00
5	$ 37.50	Win $ 5.50
6	$ 45.00	Win $ 13.00
7	$ 52.50	Win $ 20.50

Let's analyze the above chart.

The dilemma of the CRAP player ! ! !

When, oh when, should we remove our Place Bets ?

The answer is very obvious. Enjoy two wins for a $ 15 profit and ***then remove all Place bets.*** Now we have protected the $ 15 profit for this shooter. Going for broke, after four more wins (making a total of six wins), only gives you a net win of $ 13. This is $ 2 LESS than only two wins. Can this be ? Let me say it again: going for broke, or letting the six place bets (4, 5, 6, 8, 9, 10) remain active until the deadly singular 7 shows up, is not a good idea. We are much better off with two wins than six wins. In fact, if the Gods Of Fate would favor us with seven wins, our net gain would only be $20.50 or $5.50 more than only two wins.

Soon to be published is my book on "Casino CRAPS — Probabilities and Odds", which contains some really fascinating information.

Without delving into derivations, allow me merely to present certain facts about the probability of two wins, six wins and seven wins for the six place bets (4, 5, 6, 8, 9,10).

* Number of Wins	Probability	Odds to Win	Odds Against Winning
2	0.64000	** 1.78	
6	0.26214		** 2.81
7	0.20972		3.77

* Before the fatal seven.
** Odds to one.

Besides the practicality of earning more with two wins than with six wins on our six place bets, another sound reason for two wins rather than six or seven wins is found when analyzing the results of the probabilities of these wins. The probabilities of two wins, six wins and seven wins converts into the odds of making two wins and the odds against making six and seven wins.

It's great knowing the odds of winning two times on the six Place bets is in our favor (1.78 to 1), but the odds against six wins are 2.81 **against** our favor. For seven wins the odds **against** this occurring are 3.77 to 1.

This is one of the reasons why CRAP players end up in the financial CRAP-per.

Allow me to digress. Almost 18 months ago, when I began compiling articles about this very fascinating game of CRAPS, I learned some interesting facts. One of my first new disclosures was that by combining various place bets the casino's win percentages decreased dramatically. To obtain an opinion how the unknowing gambling public, authors and CRAP experts would react to my new findings, I presented my calculations to one of the most renowned casino executives. He brought along an expert on various table games, especially CRAPS. After reviewing my presentation, they both agreed: "Zeke, these are only numbers. What do numbers have to do with those crazy DICE ?"

I REST MY CASE.

36 PROBABILITY TABLE

Number	Possibilities
2	1
3	2
4	3
5	4
6	5
7	6
8	5
9	4
10	3
11	2
12	1
	36 COMBINATIONS

Two Six Sided Cubes Can Generate
36 Different Combinations of Numbers

From the 36 Probability Table we create the 1980 Probability by multiplying 36 x 55 to obtain 1980. This is the smallest number to obtain the various **Casino's win percentages** on every possible CRAP wager without using fractions.

Right Bettor's 1980 Probability Table

Come Out Rolls	Winners		Losers		
Eleven (11)	110				
Seven (7)	330				
Two (2)			55		
Three (3)			110		
Twelve (12)			55		
Come Out Rolls =	440	+	220	=	660

Point Numbers	Winners		Losers		
Four (4)	55		110		
Ten (10)	55		110		
Five (5)	88		132		
Nine (9)	88		132		
Six (6)	125		150		
Eight (8)	125		150		
Points =	536	+	784	=	1320
					1980

Total Losses = 220 + 784 = 1004
Total Wins = 440 + 536 = 976

Excess Losses = 28

$\frac{28}{1980}$ = 1.414% **Casino's win percentage** for Pass Line and Come Bet wagers

Wrong Bettor's 1980 Probability Table

Come Out Rolls		Winners		Losers		
Eleven (11)				110		
Seven (7)				330		
Two (2)		55				
Three (3)		110				
*Twelve (12)		*Stand-off*				
Come Out Rolls	=	165	+	440	=	605
Point Number						
Four (4)		110		55		
Ten (10)		110		55		
Five (5)		132		88		
Nine (9)		132		88		
Six (6)		150		125		
Eight (8)		150		125		
Points	=	784	+	536	=	1320
						1925 *

Total Losses = 440 + 536 = 976
Total Wins = 165 + 784 = 949

Excess Losses = 27

$\frac{27}{1925}$ = 1.40259 % **Casino's win percentage** for Don't Pass Line and Don't Come wagers

* (1980) - 55 for standoff #12 = 1925 *

ZEKE'S BEST BETS

Place Bets	Casino's %	Players Insurance Factor (wins / losses)
6-8	1.042	1.67
* 5-6-8-9	1.136	3.00
5-6-8	1.176	2.33
9-6-8	1.176	2.33
** 5-6-8-9	1.181	3.00
*** 4-5-6-8-9-10	1.250	4.00
**** 4-5-6-8-9-10	1.296	4.00
5-6-9	1.645	2.17
5-8-9	1.645	2.17

* When wagers are multiples of $ 22 total for all inside numbers

** When wagers are multiples of $ 30 for each of the inside numbers

*** When wagers are multiples of $ 32 total for all numbers

**** When wagers are multiples of $ 30 for each of the numbers

REMOVE ALL PLACE BETS AFTER (1) WIN

CASINO'S ADVANTAGE ON EVERY POSSIBLE INDIVIDUAL CRAP BET

	Casino's Percentage
Don't Pass w D-Odds	0.459 %
Pass w D-Odds	0.606
Don't Pass w S-Odds	0.691
Don't Come w S-Odds	0.691
Pass w S-Odds	0.848
Come w S-Odds	0.848
Don't Pass	1.403
Pass	1.414
Don't Come	1.403
Come	1.414
Place Bet 6	1.515
Place Bet 8	1.515
Field, db. 2; trpl.12	2.78
Place Bet 5	4.00
Place Bet 9	4.00
Field, db. 2; dbl.12	5.56
Place Bet 4	6.67
Place Bet 10	6.67
Six	9.09
Eight	9.09
Hardway 6	9.09
Hardway 8	9.09
Hardway 4	11.11
Hardway 10	11.11
Any Crap	11.11
Eleven (16 for 1)	11.11
Three (16 for 1)	11.11
Two (31 for 1)	13.89
Twelve (31 for 1)	13.89
Eleven (15 for 1)	16.67
Three (15 for 1)	16.67
Two (30 for 1)	16.67
Twelve (30 for 1)	16.67
Seven (5 for 1)	16.67
Under 7 (1 for 1)	16.67
Over 7 (1 for 1)	16.67

All of these percentages are without the benefit of Zeke's Techniques

PASS LINE WAGERS VERSUS PLACE BETS

Compare the following casino's win percentages ***once point number is established.***

WAGER		CASINO'S WIN PERCENTAGE%	
Inside Place Bets (5, 6, 8, 9)		**1.136**	
Pass Line Wager	(weighted)	18.79	No Odds
Pass Line Wager	(4 or 10)	33.33	No Odds
Pass Line Wager	(5 or 9)	20.00	No Odds
Pass Line Wager	(6 or 8)	9.09	No Odds
Pass Line Wager	(4 or 10)	16.67	Single Odds
* Pass Line Wager	(5 or 9)	10.00	Single Odds
** Pass Line Wager	(5 or 9)	9.09	Single Odds
Pass Line Wager	(6 or 8)	4.54	Single Odds
Pass Line Wager	(4 or 10)	11.11	Double Odds
Pass Line Wager	(5 or 9)	6.67	Double Odds
Pass Line Wager	(6 or 8)	3.03	Double Odds

NOT OVERLY ACCURATE BUT GOOD ENOUGH

A few weeks before this book went to press I spent more than eleven plus hours (over 9 sessions) analyzing the formats various stickpersons used in presenting the dice to the shooter.

The total numbers generated were1724. This was approximately 154 tosses per hour. A little higher than normal, but a goodly portion was monitored at $25 and $100 minimum tables. This is where much less time consuming proposition wagers are made.

I do not consider the following observations as overly accurate. This is because the 30 different stickpersons observed, only represent a miniscule percentage of all stickpersons. Actually it is estimated only twenty-odd (no play on words) different stickpersons participated. Observations of 200 to 300 non-identical stickpersons may have a completely different obtuse conclusions. Nevertheless, here are the results:

(a) There were 445 come-out-rolls. All of the available dice were presented, generally after a "shuffle-act" by stickperson towards the shooter. To my pleasant surprise 121 pre-set the dice for the come-out-roll. Most of these pre-setters had two box cars (6-6) on the top surfaces, or elevens (6-5), or sevens (1-6, 2-5, 4-3). I am not exactly certain, but probably 10 % to 15 % of these pre-setters also pre-set vertical surfaces. I'm not positive as many threw the dice quickly or the view was obstructed by their fingers.

(b) If the come-out rolls were natural winners (7-11) or craps (2, 3, 12) the stickperson generally presented the dice to the shooter with either the 7 or 11 dice totals, but there were exceptions.

(c) Once the point number was established, the stickperson presented the dice to the shooter with the dice totals of the previous toss eighty percent of the time, UNLESS the previous toss was a craps. Twenty percent changed the dice totals. The number of pre-setters were considerably less once the point number was established, only 32 instead of 121 (32 and 121 are incidents not people).

(d) When two like numbers were the pre-sets, then almost one-eighth of the time the next toss resulted in a hardway number. This is better than the one-ninth theoretically expected.

(e) The shooters that pre-set the dice on the come-out-roll had almost 20 % more 7's and 11's than theoretically expected, But I, a believer in pre-sets, must be honest and say that the amount of dice totals generated is too low to prove a point. If any vertical pre-sets were made, the come-out-roll pre-set addicts generally were the guilty parties.

(f) About eighty percent of the time shooters picked up the dice as presented and tossed them. On one occasion four consecutive fives were generated, each after being presented by the stickman with four different dice totals. And not one being a five. This is why I state that as interesting as the eleven plus hours were, the total of 1724 generated numbers is too miniscule to properly evaluate.

Readers, the little wisdom we obtain from the 1724 numbers generated is somewhat useful. Bear in mind NO ONE has attempted any analysis before, therefore this information is better than none.

In the future we will attempt a more reasonable length of time accomplishing this experiment. Possibly 400 hours (approximately 55,000 dice totals), but even then this will be only a small part in the scheme of things and will entail enlisting many observers.

NOTE: Once a point number was established, it was observed that if the point number or its complement (5 is the complement to 9, etc.) was not presented to the shooters then the most popular dice arrangement presented was the 4 - 2.

CRITICISM ON NUMBERS, PERCENTAGES, SUPERSTITIONS, and WHITE SPACE

I am grateful for the many positive remarks I have received about the first two books published.

There have, of course, been other remarks that literally lambasted these books. Quite a few were adamant that the statement numbers and percentages have nothing to do with those erratic dice ! Others actually cursed and questioned my intelligence when the subject of superstition was used in Zeke's Techniques. Two readers actually questioned my honesty for using too much areas of white space in my first two books.

I won't even attempt to respond.

But if any reader wants to discuss a technical issue, my time is your time.

Send your question along with a self-addressed stamp envelope to:

Hi-Lo-Yo Publishing
P.O. Box 3066B
Margate, NJ 08402-3066

Attn: Zeke Feinberg

and you will receive a prompt reply. If you disagree with my findings, let me know why. If you don't understand my views and need a better explanation, let me know.

ZEKE'S ANALYSIS OF WHO ZEKE APPRECIATES

Dealers and Stickpersons	95 %
Box Persons	50 %
Floor Persons	35 %
Senior Floor Persons	20 %
Upper Casino Executives	10 %

These marks are not for liking or disliking, but show the regard I have for those in these positions. This is really a grade for many non-doers. Most are afraid of their own shadow, or should I say their superior's shadow. There are so many constructive ways the casinos various operations can be improved, but why should they rock the boat ?

TWENTY-FOUR SUCCESSIVE FULL PRESS PLACE BETS AND THEN WE ARE LAUGHING AT THE SEVEN

Probability of twenty-four wins on the 5 - 6 - 8 - 9 place bets:

$$= 0.75$$

Probability of 24 wins before one seven = $(0.75)^{24}$

$$P = 0.00100339$$

ODDS AGAINST 24 WINS BEFORE 1 SEVEN are:

996 to 1

Casino Pay-off, if place bets are fully pressed to double next wager is:

80 to 1

Pay-off is only 8 % of true odds ! ! !

ASSUMPTIONS:

(1) The twenty-four (24) wins were equally divided on the four inside numbers. Wagers were doubled each time and the odd dollars were added to profits.

(2) After the twenty-fourth hit, somebody up there whispered, "Take them down now. I have to send Devila, one of the evilest sevens !" So, all the place bets, with their sprouting profits, were removed to safety — the chip rack.

(3) The original wagers were: $25 each on the 5 and 9, $30 each on the 6 and 8. $110 total on the inside numbers:

Payoffs were $35 for all four numbers.

PLACE BETS 6 OR 8

Original Wager $ 30

Win #		Odd Dollar Profit	New Wager
Win # 1	- $ 35	$ 5	60
2	- $ 70	10	120
3	- $ 140	20	240
4	- $ 280	40	480
5	- $ 560	80	960
6	- $ 1120		
		$ 155	

Net Win = ($1120 + $960 + $155) - $30

= $2235 - $30 = $2205

PLACE BETS 5 OR 9

Original Wager = $25

	Odd Dollar Profit	New Wager
Win # 1 - $ 35	$ 10	$ 50
2 - $ 70	20	100
3 - $ 140	40	200
4 - $ 280	80	400
5 - $ 560	160	800
6 - $ 1120		
	$ 310	

Net Win = ($1120 + $800 + $310) - $30

= $2230 - $25 = $2205

RESUME:

Net Win on 6 = $ 2205
Net Win on 8 = 2205
Net Win on 5 = 2205
Net Win on 9 = 2205

NET WIN = $ 8820

Investment = $ 110

Net Win Factor $= \frac{\$ 8820}{\$ 110} = 80.2$

or 80 to 1

Here we go again ! ! !

FACTS:

The player had 24 successive wins on the four inside numbers. The 24 wins were equally divided. Each time the player DOUBLED WAGER, taking down as profit the odd dollars.

Miraculously the player by-passed Devila, one of the most dreadful, horrendous and devilish sevens, by removing the place bets.

RESULTS:	Winnings	1	$ 5000	chip
		3	$ 1000	chips
		8	$ 100	chips
		4	$ 5	chips
			$ 8920	
	.Investment	1	$ 100	chip
		2	$ 5	chips
Total Return after Removal			$ 8930	

Original Investment	$ 110
Dollar Win Factor	80 to 1
Probability against 24 wins	996 to 1

Ladies and Gentlemen:
This is why the casinos love the place bet press bettors. They will be comped to comp kingdom come.

Do you really believe what those idiotic authors say —

"The casinos FEAR the players who PRESS and PRESS and PRESS and fade away, like old soldiers.

These results are BAD ENOUGH,

BUT

The astronomical odds of the player removing the overloaded place bet wagers BEFORE the fatal 7 appears is beyond my computations.

Probability against making 24 wins	=	996 to 1
Dollar win factor pay off	=	80 to 1

$$\frac{996}{80} = \frac{12.45}{1}$$

What does this signify ?

It means this oh-so-lucky player is receiving less than one-twelfth of his due rewards. In spite of the overwhelming odds that the place bets are removed expeditiously, the player's business agent is taking almost 92 % of the potential revenue. And who is the business agent no one but the double-edged casino itself.

If a player had attempted one more win (25th) and a 7 was generated, then the press bettor will have profits of ONLY $1780, for an original investment of $110.

REPEAT: After 24 consecutive fully pressed (double each new wager after a win) wins, but failing on the 25th attempt, the net profit would be $1780 for an original investment of $110. This equates to only a 16 to 1 return, as compared to 996 to 1 odds against having 24 inside place bet wins before one seven.

The previous analysis for the 24 place bet wins (before the one deadly 7) had an original investment of $110 on the four inside numbers ($25 each on the 5 and 9, with the 6 and 8 having wagers of $30 each). The tremendous majority of CRAP players are five cents and ten cents players ($5 and $10). Therefore if they were the recipients of these 24 consecutive "inside" wins before the singular 7, their respective wins would have been:

Wager	Win
$ 22 on the inside numbers	$ 1764
$ 44 on the inside numbers	$ 3528

And many imbecilic CRAP experts and authors claim the casinos are deathly afraid of these nickel and dime players.

Contrary to this belief, the casino would welcome such a winner so others could be lured into their 'Den of Iniquity', the Arena of Crap Action.

SPECIAL: When place betting the 5 or 9 for $25 and the 6 or 8 for $30, whenever you press these wagers fully the final profit (or theoretical profit) will be equal for both sets. The dollar win factor is higher for the 5 or 9 as the initial investment is lower ($25 vs $30).

Why I Write Books about the Game of CRAPS

Many years ago I decided to spend weekends in the solitude of New Jersey shores and write several books. One book is about my memoirs and business experiences and observations. Another was to be a first in a series of books about numbers, arithmetic and mathematics for children.

As fascinating as I found the art of writing, I decided to take periodic recesses from pen-in-hand at the Crap tables in the Atlantic City casinos. Before and during the Second World War I had experienced the street art of CRAPS. Fascinating game that it is, I never played seriously. To me it was FUN TIME only. In fact, one time at the old Golden Nugget casino (now Bally Grand) four business associates saw me at a CRAP table. All four came up to me holding bundles of $500, $100 and $25 chips. "Zeke, what are you doing playing at a three dollar table ?" "Very simple, I can't find a two dollar table!"

As I was playing and charting, (or just charting), I observed that very few people were winning any money. I corresponded with the New Jersey Casino Commission, then located in Laurenceville, NJ and obtained data regarding all table games and the slots. The results shocked me. The public was throwing money into the SEWER.

I am a reader and over the years I have read many books. One percent would be fictional. I have read Scarne's Book on Gambling. I then reread it and many others about CRAPS. They all read alike, but everyone was still losing money. Why ?

I investigated the Game of CRAPS with an open mind. I could not believe what I had discovered. Every author followed the same path that the late Scarne created. Everyone copied his mistakes, even in certain win percentages. Some incorporated money management systems, certain disciplines, various methods and techniques BUT no one really gave any deep thought to the game of CRAPS.

I now blazoning state that 99 % of the CRAP players, so-called experts, and other CRAP authors, not to mention casino personnel ***Do Not Really Understand The Game Of Craps.***

This is why my book had to be written.

BALLY'S GRAND

for the month of May, 1992

Casino Revenues	Authorized Units	Win	Drop	Win Percentage
Table Game				
Blackjack	53	3,062,640	20,476,324	15.0 %
Craps	14	1,789,687	12,369,872	14.5 %
Roulette	10	651,081	2,905,899	22.4 %
Big Six	3	132,577	270,289	49.1 %
Baccarat	2	(124,003)	3,500,171	-3.5 %
Minibaccarat	2	165,304	1,007,142	16.4 %
Other (Red Dog & Sic Bo)	4	135,171	479,468	28.2 %
Total - Table Games	**88**	**5,812,457**	**41,009,165**	**14.2 %**
Coin Oper Machines			Handle	
$ .05 Slot Machines	69	260,894	1,787,205	14.6 %
$ .25 Slot Machines	476	3,196,552	23,513,715	13.6 %
$1.00 Slot Machines	195	2,118,158	21,177,683	10.0 %
Other Slot Machines	697	5,742,677	70,495,740	8.1 %
Total - Coin Oper. Machines	**1437**	**11,318,281**	**116,974,343**	**9.7 %**
Total Casino Revenues		**$ 17,130,738**		

BALLY'S PARK PLACE

for the month of May, 1992

Casino Revenues	Authorized Units	Win	Drop	Win Percentage
Table Game				
Blackjack	72	3,954,486	23,967,992	16.5 %
Craps	14	1,265,553	10,925,397	11.6 %
Roulette	12	1,134,710	4,188,536	27.1 %
Big Six	4	247,946	524,219	47.3 %
Baccarat	2	141,203	2,773,374	5.1 %
Minibaccarat	2	326,649	1,492,678	21.9 %
Other (Red Dog & Sic Bo)	4	182,368	584,722	31.2 %
Total - Table Games	**110**	**7,252,915**	**44,456,918**	**16.3 %**
Coin Oper Machines			Handle	
$ .05 Slot Machines	83	391,166	2,415,232	16.2 %
$ .25 Slot Machines	684	5,276,894	41,112,377	12.8 %
$1.00 Slot Machines	251	3,767,923	42,865,260	8.8 %
Other Slot Machines	793	8,583,914	94,216,457	9.1 %
Total - Coin Oper. Machines	**1811**	**18,019,897**	**180,609,326**	**10.0 %**
Total Casino Revenues		**$ 25,272,812**		

CAESARS ATLANTIC CITY

for the month of May, 1992

Casino Revenues	Authorized Units	Win	Drop	Win Percentage
Table Game				
Blackjack	57	4,408,354	29,566,512	14.9 %
Craps	16	4,131,518	26,014,597	15.9 %
Roulette	11	756,489	7,531,530	10.0 %
Big Six	2	165,789	386,787	42.9 %
Baccarat	3	(496,639)	9,352,140	-5.3 %
Minibaccarat	2	341,352	1,565,153	21.8 %
Other (Red Dog & Sic Bo)	5	256,290	987,525	26.0 %
Total - Table Games	**96**	**9,563,153**	**75,404,244**	**12.7 %**
Coin Oper Machines			Handle	
$ .05 Slot Machines	34	153,178	1,000,025	15.3 %
$ .25 Slot Machines	449	3,790,546	25,699,449	14.7 %
$1.00 Slot Machines	419	4,141,958	47,155,830	8.8 %
Other Slot Machines	815	8,279,545	88,470,994	9.4 %
Total - Coin Oper. Machines	**1717**	**16,365,227**	**162,326,298**	**10.1 %**
Total Casino Revenues		**$ 25,928,380**		

CLARIDGE HOTEL & CASINO

for the month of May, 1992

Casino Revenues	Authorized Units	Win	Drop	Win Percentage
Table Game				
Blackjack	44	1,561,568	12,263,321	12.7 %
Craps	10	1,000,663	8,299,768	12.1 %
Roulette	6	436,077	1,598,987	27.3 %
Big Six	1	56,344	147,678	38.2 %
Baccarat	1	31,026	492,746	6.3 %
Minibaccarat	1	56,285	390,025	14.4 %
Other (Red Dog & Sic Bo)	3	65,134	185,135	35.2 %
Total - Table Games	**66**	**3,207,097**	**23,377,660**	**13.7 %**
Coin Oper Machines			Handle	
$ .05 Slot Machines	69	252,543	1,621,954	15.6 %
$ .25 Slot Machines	443	3,540,237	26,908,063	13.2 %
$1.00 Slot Machines	189	1,652,266	14,554,299	11.4 %
Other Slot Machines	664	4,354,957	42,655,554	10.2 %
Total - Coin Oper. Machines	**1365**	**9,800,003**	**85,739,870**	**11.4 %**
Total Casino Revenues		**$ 13,007,100**		

HARRAH'S CASINO HOTEL

for the month of May, 1992

Casino Revenues	Authorized Units	Win	Drop	Win Percentage
Table Game				
Blackjack	57	3,096,486	20,777,593	14.9 %
Craps	16	2,149,856	15,032,062	14.3 %
Roulette	18	1,052,290	4,110,354	25.6 %
Big Six	2	60,042	175,151	34.3 %
Baccarat	2	199,826	707,544	28.2 %
Minibaccarat	2	95,347	458,811	20.8 %
Other (Red Dog & Sic Bo)	7	187,062	620,682	30.1 %
Total - Table Games	**104**	**6,840,909**	**41,882,197**	**16.3 %**
Coin Oper Machines			Handle	
$ .05 Slot Machines	47	195,092	1,238,939	15.7 %
$ .25 Slot Machines	560	4,626,275	44,136,083	10.5 %
$1.00 Slot Machines	323	4,001,815	48,974,300	8.2 %
Other Slot Machines	988	9,852,096	126,353,819	7.8 %
Total - Coin Oper. Machines	**1918**	**18,675,278**	**220,703,141**	**8.5 %**
Total Casino Revenues		**$ 25,516,187**		

MERV GRIFFIN'S RESORTS

for the month of May, 1992

Casino Revenues	Authorized Units	Win	Drop	Win Percentage
Table Game				
Blackjack	60	3,105,387	21,797,864	14.2 %
Craps	16	2,619,836	17,857,695	14.7 %
Roulette	13	862,594	3,071,795	28.1 %
Big Six	2	132,539	290,522	45.6 %
Baccarat	2	302,015	2,534,124	11.9 %
Minibaccarat	2	75,838	845,786	9.0 %
Other (Red Dog & Sic Bo)	4	109,979	434,867	25.3 %
Total - Table Games	**99**	**7,208,188**	**46,832,653**	**15.4 %**
Coin Oper Machines			Handle	
$ .05 Slot Machines	70	218,528	1,426,741	15.3 %
$ .25 Slot Machines	640	4,724,033	37,443,589	12.6 %
$1.00 Slot Machines	195	2,513,069	27,756,915	9.1 %
Other Slot Machines	778	6,552,026	74,666,920	8.8 %
Total - Coin Oper. Machines	**1683**	**14,007,656**	**141,294,165**	**9.9 %**
Total Casino Revenues		**$ 21,215,844**		

SANDS HOTEL AND CASINO

for the month of May, 1992

Casino Revenues	Authorized Units	Win	Drop	Win Percentage
Table Game				
Blackjack	53	3,586,603	25,606,623	14.0 %
Craps	16	1,869,137	15,209,576	12.3 %
Roulette	13	1,654,537	4,618,157	35.8 %
Big Six	2	107,925	230,004	46.9 %
Baccarat	4	1,398,409	8,860,726	15.8 %
Minibaccarat	2	180,698	1,327,683	13.6 %
Other (Red Dog & Sic Bo)	1	130,522	513,172	25.4 %
Total - Table Games	**91**	**8,927,831**	**56,365,941**	**15.8 %**
Coin Oper Machines			Handle	
$ .05 Slot Machines	0			
$ .25 Slot Machines	448	3,521,221	25,247,762	13.9 %
$1.00 Slot Machines	216	2,252,046	22,822,507	9.9 %
Other Slot Machines	796	6,147,823	71,982,078	8.5 %
Total - Coin Oper. Machines	**1460**	**11,921,090**	**120,052,347**	**9.9 %**
Total Casino Revenues		**$ 20,848,921**		

SHOWBOAT

for the month of May, 1992

Casino Revenues	Authorized Units	Win	Drop	Win Percentage
Table Game				
Blackjack	49	3,044,461	18,856,489	16.1 %
Craps	16	2,348,478	15,742,077	14.9 %
Roulette	8	600,737	2,631,623	22.8 %
Big Six	1	94,764	219,818	43.1 %
Baccarat	3	556,785	3,008,913	18.5 %
Minibaccarat	2	52,017	433,551	12.0 %
Other (Red Dog & Sic Bo)	1	19,599	138,635	14.1 %
Total - Table Games	**80**	**6,716,841**	**41,031,106**	**16.4 %**
Coin Oper Machines			Handle	
$ .05 Slot Machines	87	340,690	2,252,389	15.1 %
$ .25 Slot Machines	667	5,523,718	49,590,226	11.1 %
$1.00 Slot Machines	206	2,538,381	29,289,326	8.7 %
Other Slot Machines	917	8,149,379	93,797,633	8.7 %
Total - Coin Oper. Machines	**1877**	**16,552,168**	**174,929,574**	**9.5 %**
Total Casino Revenues		**$ 23,269,009**		

TROPWORLD CASINO AND ENTERTAINMENT RESORT

for the month of May, 1992

Casino Revenues	Authorized Units	Win	Drop	Win Percentage
Table Game				
Blackjack	75	3,161,555	23,880,994	13.2 %
Craps	16	2,235,319	13,968,184	16.0 %
Roulette	16	821,258	4,184,172	19.6 %
Big Six	3	128,193	228,080	56.2 %
Baccarat	3	489,381	2,209,034	22.2 %
Minibaccarat	2	397,852	1,656,657	24.0 %
Other (Red Dog & Sic Bo)	7	174,817	541,802	32.3 %
Total - Table Games	**122**	**7,408,375**	**46,668,923**	**15.9 %**
Coin Oper Machines			Handle	
$ .05 Slot Machines	51	164,216	968,622	17.0 %
$ .25 Slot Machines	545	3,684,492	29,768,672	12.4 %
$1.00 Slot Machines	292	3,743,835	47,844,988	7.8 %
Other Slot Machines	1,578	12,775,939	166,455,346	7.7 %
Total - Coin Oper. Machines	**2466**	**20,368,482**	**245,037,628**	**8.3 %**
Total Casino Revenues		**$ 27,776,857**		

TRUMP CASTLE

for the month of May, 1992

Casino Revenues	Authorized Units	Win	Drop	Win Percentage
Table Game				
Blackjack	53	2,681,485	19,014,759	14.1 %
Craps	16	2,911,022	15,900,132	18.3 %
Roulette	10	681,452	2,726,831	25.0 %
Big Six	1	59,405	140,365	42.3 %
Baccarat	3	205,626	2,861,962	7.2 %
Minibaccarat	2	21,207	1,116,214	1.9 %
Other (Red Dog & Sic Bo)	4	119,449	488,401	24.5 %
Total - Table Games	**89**	**6,679,566**	**42,248,664**	**15.8 %**
Coin Oper Machines			Handle	
$ .05 Slot Machines	49	215,596	1,351,191	16.0 %
$ .25 Slot Machines	526	3,421,260	28,852,352	11.9 %
$1.00 Slot Machines	244	2,264,247	24,088,588	9.4 %
Other Slot Machines	900	6,976,305	79,457,666	8.8 %
Total - Coin Oper. Machines	**1719**	**12,877,408**	**133,749,797**	**9.6 %**
Total Casino Revenues		**$ 19,556,974**		

TRUMP PLAZA

for the month of May, 1992

Casino Revenues	Authorized Units	Win	Drop	Win Percentage
Table Game				
Blackjack	56	3,483,893	30,235,734	11.5 %
Craps	13	1,419,533	12,575,833	11.3 %
Roulette	13	1,473,202	5,297,473	27.8 %
Big Six	2	186,216	391,491	47.6 %
Baccarat	3	(626,846)	12,501,457	-5.0 %
Minibaccarat	4	464,566	3,026,896	15.3 %
Other (Red Dog & Sic Bo)	4	233,754	799,385	28.0 %
Total - Table Games	**95**	**6,624,318**	**64,828,269**	**10.2 %**
Coin Oper Machines			Handle	
$ .05 Slot Machines	81	321,251	2,004,720	16.0 %
$ .25 Slot Machines	531	4,221,209	32,848,408	12.9 %
$1.00 Slot Machines	220	2,875,829	32,859,581	8.8 %
Other Slot Machines	890	7,333,826	86,713,174	8.5 %
Total - Coin Oper. Machines	**1722**	**14,752,115**	**154,425,883**	**9.6 %**
Total Casino Revenues		**$ 21,376,433**		

TRUMP TAJ MAHAL CASINO RESORT

for the month of May, 1992

Casino Revenues	Authorized Units	Win	Drop	Win Percentage
Table Game				
Blackjack	96	6,305,624	42,680,439	14.8 %
Craps	24	3,662,564	25,308,511	14.5 %
Roulette	21	1,301,315	6,083,547	21.4 %
Big Six	6	328,649	673,562	48.8 %
Baccarat	4	1,405,279	11,468,186	12.3 %
Minibaccarat	2	408,395	2,411,039	16.9 %
Other (Red Dog & Sic Bo)	4	241,300	741,731	32.5 %
Total - Table Games	**157**	**13,653,126**	**89,367,015**	**15.3 %**
Coin Oper Machines			Handle	
$ .05 Slot Machines	156	582,236	3,805,788	15.3 %
$ .25 Slot Machines	1235	8,278,524	67,476,332	12.3 %
$1.00 Slot Machines	294	3,414,956	41,936,024	8.1 %
Other Slot Machines	1099	9,656,985	111,338,426	8.7 %
Total - Coin Oper. Machines	**2784**	**21,932,701**	**224,556,570**	**9.8 %**
Total Casino Revenues		**$ 35,585,827**		

Look for these other exciting new books by Zeke Feinberg in your bookstore soon

CASINO CRAPS - EARN $12 TO $24 PER HOUR PLAYING CASINO CRAPS - Beat The Recession

CASINO CRAPS IS A VICIOUS $ $ DEVOURING GAME - Cutting The Crap Out Of Craps

CASINO CRAPS CHATTER - A Series of 3 books

CASINO CRAPS - FOR HIGH ROLLERS

CASINO CRAPS - PLACE BETS & VIGORISH

CASINO CRAPS - HORNS, WHIRLS, HI-LO-YO, CRAPS & HARDWAYS

CASINO CRAPS - WOEFUL PASS LINE BETTOR and the PARADOX of the WRONG BETTOR

CASINO CRAPS - For NOVICE PLAYERS
Casino Craps is not for gambling.
Casino Craps is for exciting entertainment

CASINO CRAPS - PROBABILITIES & ODDS

CASINO CRAPS - LIVE CASINO ACTION
Financial results using many different methods

SIC-BO